THE 100

ABSOLUTELY UNBREAKABLE

LAWS OF
BUSINESS
SUCCESS

Books authored by Brian Tracy:

Advanced Selling Strategies

Great Little Book on Effective Leadership

Great Little Book on the Gift of Self-Confidence

The Great Big Book of Wisdom

Little Silver Book of Prosperity

Great Little Book on Mastering Your Time

Maximum Achievement

The Peak Performance Woman

Great Little Book on Personal Achievement

Success Is a Journey

Great Little Book on Successful Selling

A Treasury of Personal Achievement

Great Little Book on the Universal Laws of Success

Maximum Achievement Goal Planner

Hire and Keep the Best People

Focal Point

Get Paid More and Promoted Faster

Eat that Frog!

The 21 Success Secrets of Self-Made Millionaires

Book coathored by Brian Tracy:

Speaking Secrets of the Masters

The Traits of Champions

THE 100
ABSOLUTELY UNBREAKABLE
LAWS OF BUSINESS SUCCESS

BRIAN TRACY

BERRETT-KOEHLER PUBLISHERS, INC.
San Francisco

Berrett-Koehler Publishers, Inc.
235 Montgomery Street, Suite 650
San Francisco, CA 94104-2916
Tel: (415) 288-0260 Fax: (415) 362-2512   www.bkconnection.com

ORDERING INFORMATION

Quantity sales. Special discounts are available on quantity purchases by corporations, associations, and others. For details, contact the "Special Sales Department" at the Berrett-Koehler address above.

Individual sales. Berrett-Koehler publications are available through most bookstores. They can also be ordered direct from Berrett-Koehler: Tel: (800) 929-2929; Fax: (802) 864-7626; www.bkconnection.com

Orders for college textbook/course adoption use. Please contact Berrett-Koehler: Tel: (800) 929-2929; Fax: (802) 864-7626.

Orders by U.S. trade bookstores and wholesalers. Please contact Publishers Group West, 1700 Fourth Street, Berkeley, CA 94710. Tel: (510) 528-1444; Fax (510) 528-3444.

Printed in the United States of America

Library of Congress Cataloging-in-Publication Data

Tracy, Brian.
The 100 absolutely unbreakable laws of business success / author, Brian Tracy.
    p.   cm.
    Includes bibliographical references and index.
    ISBN 1-57675-126-0
    1. Success in business. 2. Entrepreneurship—Psychological aspects. I.
Title: Hundred absolutely unbreakable laws of business success. II. Title.
    HF5386.T8139 2000
    650.1—dc21   00-26693
First Hardcover Edition 2000
First Paperback Edition 2002

07 06 05 04 03 02   10 9 8 7 6 5 4 3 2 1

Copyediting and proofreading: PeopleSpeak
Interior design and production: Marin Bookworks
Cover design: Camille Woodbury
Indexing: Leonard Rosenbaum

Dedication

—ᵐ—

This book is dedicated to my son Michael Tracy. May these timeless truths guide and inspire you to the wonderful life in business that stretches before you.

Table of Contents

—⟋⟍—

Preface

—m—

Once upon a time, I set out on a lifelong journey to find out why the world works the way it does. Like many people on this journey, I found my way into sales, then management, and eventually entrepreneurship and business building. Over time, I began to notice consistent and predictable patterns and principles that seemed to accompany all business success. Listing and explaining them is the purpose of this book.

My mission in life has been the same for more than twenty-five years. It is to liberate individual potential by giving people ideas and strategies they can use to get more of the benefits and rewards they want far faster than they would without these ideas.

I believe that life is the most precious and wonderful of all gifts. With this belief, I have been driven for years to find ways to reduce the amount of life you need to spend to achieve the material and nonmaterial goals you set for yourself. Thus this book on the Laws of Business Success.

This book is written specifically for people working in the business world who want to maximize their personal potentials and get the greatest quality and quantity of business results possible in exchange for the hours, weeks, months, and years of their precious lives that they invest in their careers.

Any one of these laws can save you months and even years of hard work if you have not been living and working consistent with it up to now. And each of these laws is indispensable to your realizing your full potential. The consistent violation of any one of these laws can cost you months and even years of frustration and underachievement.

Here is a question for you: If you could earn $50,000 per year or $100,000 per year, all other things being equal, which would you choose?

The answer is obvious. You would always prefer more to less for the same amount of time and effort. And the fact is that people living by these laws and practicing these principles earn far more in the same period of time than people who do not.

These laws are similar to laws of physics, laws of mathematics, laws of mechanics, or laws of electricity. They are practical, proven laws that apply everywhere to success and business. They do not deal with health or home or love or balance or any of the great factors that make for happiness and personal fulfillment. This book does not attempt to address those issues, only the timeless principles of business success.

The best news of all regarding business success is that nature is neutral. If you do what other successful people do, you will get the results that other successful people get. And if you don't, you won't. It is as simple as that.

Some of these laws may seem simplistic or self-evident. Some repeat themselves in different ways in different categories. Don't be fooled into discounting or dismissing them on that account. Great success and mastery in any field always go to those who are "brilliant on the basics."

As you read, take a few moments with each law and honestly evaluate your own conduct and behavior with regard to that law. One insight or new idea that you did not have before can be all that it takes to change the direction of your life.

When you apply *The 100 Absolutely Unbreakable Laws of Business Success* and you live your business life in harmony with them, you will gain a distinct advantage over those who do not.

You will enjoy levels of success and satisfaction you may never have imagined possible. You will accomplish more in a few months or years than many people accomplish in a lifetime!

Brian Tracy
Solana Beach, California
March 2000

About the Author

Brian Tracy started at the bottom and worked his way up, one step at a time. He began his adult life uneducated, unskilled, and unemployed, living in his car and working at odd jobs as they came along.

At an early age, he became intensely curious about the way things work, why things happen the way they do. As he worked and traveled, read, and spoke to people, he began to discover a certain regularity and predictability in human affairs. These insights changed the direction of his life and led ultimately to the laws and ideas in this book.

Like a scientist or researcher, he tested and applied each principle, comparing his conclusions with those of others. As he worked his way from job to job, from position to position, and eventually from failure to success, he used himself as a guinea pig to prove or disprove the validity of his discoveries.

The cumulative effect of learning and applying these universal principles of success and achievement was exactly as he had predicted.

Today, Brian Tracy is one of the top business consultants in the United States and one of the most popular professional speakers in the world. He has worked with more than 500 companies of all sizes, including many in the Fortune 500. He speaks to more than 300,000 people each year worldwide on subjects of personal and corporate effectiveness.

Brian Tracy has written ten books, some of which have been translated into twelve languages. His video and audio learning programs are used worldwide to teach leadership, sales, personal success, and time management.

In addition, he has traveled and worked in eighty countries on five continents. He has a master's degree in business and administration and is an avid reader in history, philosophy, economics, religion, metaphysics, and psychology.

Brian has a wonderful way of synthesizing ideas and insights from several disciplines into practical strategies that work quickly and get fast results.

He is the president of Brian Tracy International, a consulting and training organization based in Solana Beach, California. He is married with four children and is actively involved in his community.

In this book, he shares with you his many years of wisdom distilled from his experience with people and companies across America and throughout the world.

Success Is Predictable

—ww—

This is a wonderful time to be alive. There have never been more opportunities for more people to accomplish more of their goals, both personally and professionally, than exist today. And if anything, our situation is getting better and better with each passing year.

Why is this happening? The simplest answer is that we know more today about how to achieve better results in more areas of business than we have ever known before. And this information, these ideas and insights, are like water, flowing everywhere and to everyone who is open to them and willing to use them.

The wonderful thing about information and ideas is that they are infinitely divisible. If you have an idea that can help me to be more effective in some part of my business and you share it with me, we are both enriched. If I then share this idea with someone else, and that person shares it with someone else again, everyone who receives the new idea is better off.

And knowledge is cumulative. Once it exists, it does not cease to exist. It becomes available to more and more people and it grows exponentially. Every new piece of knowledge reveals connections and interconnections with other areas of knowledge in a self-reinforcing and accelerating pattern. Each breakthrough in knowledge creates new opportunities that expand and multiply as that knowledge is exploited.

The driving force behind the explosion of knowledge and the expansion of technology is competition. This competition is more aggressive, determined, creative, and ruthless than ever before, and if anything, it will be even tougher in the months and years ahead.

It has been said that "business is war." Business books, articles, and courses are filled with references to "marketing warfare," "guerilla tactics," "counterattacks," and other military terms. And these are all true with one important distinction: the nature of the type of "war" being fought.

Military warfare is aimed at the conquest of people and territory. Business warfare is aimed at winning customers and markets. Military combat aims at destruction and victory by the use of overwhelming force. Business competition aims at finding better, faster, and cheaper ways of pleasing customers in competition with other companies that are trying to please the same customers.

This business competition is fierce. Many of the finest minds and the most talented people who have ever lived are thinking and working day and night to find ways to satisfy customers with new and better products and services. The race is on. Only those who can learn and apply the very best ideas and methods faster than their competitors will survive.

The "Winning Edge" concept says, "small differences in ability can lead to enormous differences in results." Small differences in your own personal repertoire of knowledge and skills can lead to major differences in your income and achievements.

Your aim throughout your career, for yourself and your company, should be to acquire and develop the winning edges in your field that can mean all the difference between success and mediocrity.

Today, strategies and techniques for achieving success at every level of business, and in every activity of life, are more widely available and proliferating more rapidly than at any other time in human history. And we can all benefit from them by seizing them and applying them to our lives.

The purpose of this book is to share with you a system of proven principles, or "laws," that have been discovered and rediscovered, practiced and implemented, by the most successful businesspeople everywhere, in every kind of organization, large and small, throughout the history of business enterprise. The practice of these laws will give you the winning edge.

When you know and understand these timeless truths, you will gain a tremendous advantage over those who do not. When you organize your life and business according to these universal laws and principles, you can start, build, manage, or turn around a business or department faster and easier than perhaps you ever thought possible.

The more you incorporate these principles into your daily thinking and decision making, the more effective you will become. You will attract and keep better people, produce and sell more and better products and services, control costs more intelligently, expand and grow more predictably, and increase your profits with greater consistency.

Some of these laws may sound unusual or even controversial when you first read them. Nonetheless, they are timeless truths. They have always existed. They have always worked. They are natural laws. They are embedded in the universe. In the long run, they are inviolable.

Thomas Henry Huxley wrote in *A Liberal Education*, "The chess board is the world, the pieces are the phenomena of the universe, the rules of the game are what we call the Laws of Nature. The player on the other side is hidden from us. We know that his play is always fair, just, and patient. But also we know, to our cost, that he never overlooks a mistake, or makes the smallest allowance for ignorance."

In the same way, these laws are neutral, neither positive nor negative. They are indifferent to your personal beliefs, preferences, or desires. They have always existed in business and always will. As Johann Wolfgang von Goethe wrote, "Nature understands no jesting; she is always true, always severe; she is always right, and the errors and faults are always those of man. The man incapable of appreciating her she despises and only to the apt, the pure, and true, does she resign herself and reveal her secrets."

If you want to cook, you study cooking and you follow the rules and principles regarding the combining of ingredients and preparation that have been found to work successfully in the past. You would not think to add or subtract key ingredients and expect the dish you are preparing to taste the same as if you followed the proven recipe.

By the same token, you would not expect to achieve the same business results accomplished by successful businesspeople by violating the essential laws and principles that they practice year after year.

There is a story of a man who decides to commit suicide by jumping off a thirty-story building. As he plunges toward the ground, someone leans out of a fifteenth-story window and shouts, "How's it going?"

The falling man shouts back, "So far, so good!"

Many people are living their business lives with this kind of philosophy, "So far, so good!" They are violating natural laws and principles that apply to business life, sometimes knowingly and sometimes not. Nonetheless, these truths are immutable and unavoidable. You violate them at your peril. And even if you think you are escaping their consequences in the short term, you will ultimately pay the full price that they demand.

The good news is that when you organize your life and business activities around *The 100 Absolutely Unbreakable Laws of*

Business Success, you are virtually guaranteed to enjoy success and prosperity in your business activities. Just as you reap what you sow, when you put good things in, you get good things out.

Perhaps the most important quality of a successful businessperson is pragmatism. You are pragmatic when you are not necessarily concerned about the origin of an idea. You don't ask where it comes from or who thought of it first. You ask only one question: Does it work?

You are successful in business and in life to the degree to which you find out what works and then apply that principle wherever and whenever it is appropriate to get a particular result. This book is aimed at giving you ideas and strategies that have been proven, over and over, to work.

Universal laws and principles are similar to telephone numbers in that if you dial the right number, you get through to the desired party. But even if you are brilliant, well educated, sincere, determined, and intelligent, if you dial the wrong number, you won't get through.

Year after year, thousands of companies underperform or even go out of business because either the key decision makers in those companies did not know these universal laws or they attempted to violate them and succeed anyway. Even more hundreds of thousands, and even millions, of companies fail to achieve their true potentials in sales and profitability every year because of their violation of one or more of these laws.

Remember that ignorance of the law is no excuse. Even if you do not know the laws, you are not excused from obedience to them. Even if your violation of these laws and principles is unintentional, you will still pay the full penalty in failure, frustration, and underachievement.

My Own Story

My background was not very inspiring. My family never had any money, and I paid my own way with odd jobs from the age of eleven. I left high school without graduating. After working at laboring jobs for some years, I stumbled into sales. I struggled in selling for many months until I began asking the question that changed my life: Why is it that some people are more successful than others?

The Bible says, "Seek and ye shall find, for all who seek findeth." When I began looking for the reasons why some people were doing better than I was, I began to find the answers everywhere. And when I applied the answers I found, I began to get the same results that other successful people were getting.

There is a "10/90 Rule" in life. This rule says that the first 10 percent of time that you invest in finding out the underlying laws, principles, rules, methods, and techniques of successful action in any field will save you 90 percent of the time and effort required to achieve your goals in that area.

Over the years, I have found that the smartest people are those who take the time to find out the rules of success in any area before they attempt to get results in that area. They do their homework in advance.

In my thirties, I caught up on my formal education. I participated in an Executive MBA program at a major university and received a master's degree in business and administration. I invested about 4,000 hours of my time studying business subjects and business principles. Over the years, I read hundreds of additional books and articles in my search for the so-called Secrets of Success.

When I was given an opportunity to build a sales force covering six countries, I asked the experts, read the books, listened to the audio programs, and attended the courses on recruiting and building sales organizations. Then I applied what I had learned and practiced the laws and principles that seemed to be the most effective.

In one year, I went from walking the streets, selling on straight commission, living from hand to mouth, to building a ninety-five-person sales force covering six countries and generating millions of dollars per year in revenue.

Later, when I got into real estate development, I followed the same procedure. I borrowed all the books the library had on real estate development and studied them, long into the night. I spent hours with other real estate developers, plying them with questions. Then I optioned a piece of land for $100, put together the necessary financial analyses and proposals, found a financial partner with the strength to underwrite the project, and went on to build and completely lease out a $3 million shopping center in the next twelve months.

When I began importing Japanese automobiles, I followed the same procedure. Within one year, I built a sixty-five-dealer network through which I eventually sold more than $25 million worth of vehicles.

When I became the chief operating officer of a $265 million development company, I applied to my new position the proven, tested laws, principles, and techniques that I had gathered. I completely restaffed, reorganized, and refocused the company, turning it from confusion to profitability in less than a year.

Businesspeople began to hire me as a consultant and as a troubleshooter. In company after company, I used the same procedure. I immersed myself in the business until I had ascertained the underlying "success principles" of that industry or field, and then I applied them. As a result, I was able to save or make my clients millions of dollars time after time.

I then began organizing these ideas and principles into talks and seminars for public and private audiences. Eventually, I created an entire series of seminars and training programs for individuals and businesses, many of which have now been recorded on video and audio. They are taught to businesses across America and throughout the world, in twenty languages and in thirty-one countries.

The reason that these principles, and the seminars and programs based on them, are so successful is simple. They are built around practical, proven techniques that save people years of hard work in achieving the same results. My graduates have applied the ideas they have learned toward generating hundreds of thousands and even millions of dollars of increased sales, reduced costs, or improved profits.

Over the years, working with hundreds of businesses and thousands of businesspeople, I have found that all the successful, happy, dynamic, prosperous, and growing enterprises practice these principles consistently in virtually everything they do. And when you do the same things they do, you will begin almost immediately to get the same results.

Most success in business can be easily explained by the consistent practice of these laws. Most failure can be explained by the violation or ignorance of these laws. When you align your activities with these universal principles, you will find yourself getting more and better results with less effort. You will be more relaxed and confident. You will be more optimistic and cheerful. You will be more efficient and effective.

Instead of working yourself into a state of exhaustion, only to feel frustrated and overwhelmed, you will go through enormous quantities of work quickly and easily and get far better results than other people who may be working twice as hard.

There is a simple analogy for the use of these principles that I sometimes share with my seminar audiences. I ask the question, "If you purchased a treadmill and took it home, what would determine how much benefit you got from that treadmill?" Quite quickly, the businesspeople in my audiences reply that the amount of benefit they would receive from a treadmill would be in direct proportion to how often they used it and how long they stayed on it each time.

Here is the point: There is never any question of whether or not the treadmill would help make a person fitter and healthier. Everyone knows that this is a given. The treadmill is a tested and proven device for physical fitness. This has long since been settled.

It is the same when you begin to use these tested and proven laws and principles in your own business life. The question is not whether or not they will work. The only question is how faithfully and consistently you apply them to your activities. And like a treadmill, the more often and the more consistently you apply these laws, the better they will work and the greater and easier results you will achieve.

One final point before we begin. The most common quality of successful people is they are intensely *action oriented*. They are proactive rather than reactive. They take initiative. When they hear a good idea, they act on it immediately. By taking action quickly, they immediately get feedback that enables them to self-correct and move ahead. They learn and grow from every experience. And they keep trying new things.

When you see a good idea in the pages ahead that you can apply to your work, resolve to take action on it immediately. Don't delay. One decisive action or decision to do something different can change your whole life.

The only question that should concern you is, Does it work? And these ideas work. They work virtually everywhere, under virtually all circumstances in our business system. And the more you use them, the better they will work for you. The more you align your life with these laws and principles, the happier and more successful you will be. There are no limits.

CHAPTER ONE

The Laws of Life

—⚭—

1. The Law of Cause and Effect

2. The Law of Belief

3. The Law of Expectations

4. The Law of Attraction

5. The Law of Correspondence

The Laws of Life

—◊—

Why are some people and organizations more successful than others? Why do some people have wonderful careers, moving from position to position, onward and upward, earning far more money, being consistently paid more and promoted faster?

And why is it that others go from job to job, continually worrying about money and feeling that they are unappreciated for their hard work and their contributions? Why do so many people, as Henry David Thoreau once wrote, "live lives of quiet desperation"?

When I started my business career, I was so far behind, I thought I was first. I moved from job to job, seldom by choice, a bit bewildered by the swirl of events around me and the seemingly unreasonable and unpredictable behaviors of my bosses. I felt like a pawn, playing in a game, or being *played* in a game, in which I didn't clearly understand the rules.

Then I began asking, Why are some people more successful than others?

I noticed that the people around me who were doing better than me did not seem to be smarter than me or of better character. Sometimes they had difficult personalities and questionable ethics. Often their ideas and opinions didn't make much sense. But they were doing well nonetheless.

The Great Discovery

The first big breakthrough for me was my discovery of the Aristotelian Principle of Causality, what we today call the Law of Cause and Effect. At a time when most people believed in gods on

Mount Olympus who amused themselves by toying with human fate and destiny, Aristotle stated something completely different. It changed our view of the world forever.

1. The Law of Cause and Effect

—ɷ—

Everything happens for a reason; for every effect there is a specific cause.

Aristotle asserted that we live in a world governed by law, not chance. He stated that everything happens for a reason, whether or not we know what it is. He said that every effect has a specific cause or causes. Every cause or action has an effect of some kind, whether we can see it and whether we like it or not.

This is the granddaddy law, the "Iron Law" of Western thought, of Western philosophy. The relentless search for truth, for the causal relationships among events, has led to the rise of the West in science, technology, medicine, philosophy, and even warfare for more than 2,000 years. Today this focus is driving the technological advances that are changing our world so dramatically.

This law says that achievement, wealth, happiness, prosperity, and business success are all the direct and indirect effects or results of specific causes or actions. This simply means that if you can be clear about the effect or result you want, you can probably achieve it. You can study others who have achieved the same goal, and by doing what they did, you can get the same results.

Success Is Not an Accident

Success is not a miracle, nor is it a matter of luck. Everything happens for a reason, good or bad, positive or negative. When you are absolutely clear about what you want, you only need to copy others who have achieved it before you, and you will eventually get the same results that they have.

This is referred to in the Bible as the Law of Sowing and Reaping, which says, "Whatsoever a man soweth, that also shall he reap."

Sir Isaac Newton called it the third principle of motion. He said, "For every action, there is an equal and opposite reaction."

For you and me, the most important expression of this universal law is "Thoughts are causes and conditions are effects."

Put another way, "Thought is creative." Your thoughts are the primary creative forces in your life. You create your entire world by the way you think. All the people and situations in your life have only the meaning you give them by the way you think about them. And when you change your thinking, you change your life, sometimes in seconds!

The most important principle of personal or business success is simply this: You become what you think about most of the time.

This is the great discovery upon which all religions, philosophies, metaphysics, schools of thought, and theories of psychology are based. This principle is as applicable to individuals as it is to groups of individuals and organizations. Whatever you see or experience is the expression of the thinking of the people behind the phenomenon. Ralph Waldo Emerson recognized this when he wrote, "Every great organization is merely the lengthened shadow of a single man."

 It is not what happens to you but how you think about what happens to you that determines how you feel and react. It is not the world *outside* you that dictates your circumstances or conditions. It is the world *inside* you that creates the conditions of your life.

Your Choice, Your Life

You are always free to choose. In the long run, no one forces you to think, feel, or behave the way you do. Rather, you choose your emotions and your behaviors by the way you choose to think about the world around you and about what is happening to you.

Dr. Martin Seligman of the University of Pennsylvania calls this way of reacting your "explanatory style." It is the way that you interpret or explain things to yourself. It is the critical determinant of everything you are and everything you become.

The good news is that your explanatory style is learned. This means that it can be unlearned as well. Your way of explaining things to yourself is under your control. You can interpret your experiences in such a way that you feel happy and optimistic rather than angry or frustrated. You can decide to react in such a way that your responses are constructive and effective. You are always free to choose.

Your thoughts and feelings are continually changing. They are quickly affected by the events around you. For example, when you receive a piece of good news, your attitude immediately brightens and you feel more positive toward everyone and everything. If, on the other hand, you unexpectedly receive some bad news, you can immediately become upset, angry, and short-tempered, even if the news is inaccurate or untrue. It is the way you interpret the event to yourself that determines how you react.

How you can apply this law immediately:

1. Examine the most important parts of your life—your family, your health, your work, your financial situation—and observe the cause-effect relationships between what you think, say, feel, and do and the results you are getting. Be honest with yourself.

2. Analyze how you really think about yourself in relationship to the kind of life you are living. Be absolutely honest. Consider how your thoughts in each area are causing, creating, and maintaining the situation around you. What changes could

you make in your thinking to improve the quality of some part of your life?

Four Basic Laws

Four fundamental laws flow directly from the Law of Cause and Effect. These laws underlie all the laws you will learn in this book. They explain most of the human experience, for better and for worse. All happiness and success come from living in harmony with these four laws. All unhappiness and failure comes from violating them in some way.

The big four are the Laws of Belief, Expectations, Attraction, and Correspondence. These are sublaws of the Law of Cause and Effect that explain most success and achievement, most happiness and unhappiness, most prosperity and poverty in life.

2. The Law of Belief

—〰—

Whatever you truly believe, with feeling,
becomes your reality.

You always act in a manner consistent with your beliefs, especially your beliefs about yourself. Your beliefs act like a set of filters that screen out information that is inconsistent with them. You do not necessarily believe what you see, but rather you see what you already believe. You reject information that contradicts what you have already decided to believe, whether or not your beliefs, your prejudices, are based on fact or fantasy.

The word "prejudice" means to prejudge, to reach a conclusion in advance of any information, or even in spite of information, to the contrary. One of the best success strategies of all is for you to refrain from judging other people or situations until you have enough information to make an informed decision. Especially, you must refrain from prejudging yourself and your possibilities. Your most deeply entrenched beliefs about yourself and your abilities may not be true at all.

The worst beliefs you can have are "self-limiting beliefs." These exist whenever you believe yourself to be limited in some way. For example, you may think yourself to be less talented or capable than others. You may think that others are superior to you in some way. You may have fallen into the common trap of selling yourself short and settling for far less than you are truly capable of.

These self-limiting beliefs act like brakes on your potential. They hold you back. They generate the two greatest enemies of personal success—doubt and fear. They paralyze you and cause you to hesitate to take the intelligent risks that are necessary for you to fulfill your true potential.

For you to progress, to move onward and upward in your life and your business, you must continually challenge your self-limiting beliefs. You must reject any thought or suggestion that you are limited in any way. You must accept as a basic principle that you are a "no-limit" person and that what others have done, you can do as well.

When I was a young man, coming from a difficult upbringing, I fell into the mental trap of concluding that because other people were doing better than I was, they must be better or smarter than I was. I accidentally concluded that they were worth more than I was. I must therefore be *worth less*. This false belief held me back for years.

The fact is that no one is better than you are and no one is smarter than you are. If other people are doing better, it is largely because they have developed their natural talents and abilities more than you have. They have learned the Laws of Cause and Effect that apply to their lives and work before you have. And anything anyone else has done, within reason, you can probably do as well. You just need to learn how.

How you can apply this law immediately:

1. Free your mind from doubt and fear. Imagine you have no limitations. What one great thing would you dare to dream if you knew you could not fail? If you had all the time, money, talent, skills, and contacts you could ever want, what would you decide to do or be or have in your life?

2. Challenge the self-limiting beliefs that are holding you back. Most people are blind in this area. They need the honest feedback of someone who knows them and who will be honest with them. Go to someone you know and care about and ask him or her if he or she sees any beliefs that you might have that are causing you to perform below your potential.

3. The Law of Expectations

—m—

Whatever you expect, with confidence,
becomes your own self-fulfilling prophecy.

You are always acting as a fortune-teller in your own life by the way you think and talk about how situations are going to turn out. When you confidently expect good things to happen, good things usually happen to you. If you expect negative things to happen, you are usually not disappointed.

Your expectations have an inordinate effect on the people around you as well. What you expect from people and situations determines your attitude toward them more than any other factor, and people reflect your attitude right back at you, like a mirror, whether positive or negative.

Dr. Robert Rosenthal of Harvard conducted dozens of controlled experiments over the years to test the power of the expectations of teachers on student performance. In his landmark book, *Pygmalion in the Classroom,* he tells of case after case where teachers were told that a student, or sometimes a whole class, was extremely bright and was predicted to make a quantum leap in academic performance in the coming year.

Even though the students were chosen from the school population at large, as long as the teachers believed that these students were exceptional, and the teachers expected them to do well, the students performed vastly better than other students in the same or similar classes and vastly better than could have been predicted by previous grades or behavior.

In your own personal life, your expectations of your staff, your boss, your customers, and even your future tend to come true. Your expectations exert a powerful influence on people and events, for good or for ill, so be careful!

How you can apply this law immediately:

1. Expect the best! Assume the very best of intentions on the part of your staff and coworkers. Assume from the start that they want to do a good job, make good decisions, and get good results. When things go wrong, as they do continually, instead of over-reacting, sit down with the other person in a spirit of friendliness and ask questions to determine exactly what happened. There is usually a good reason for everything.

2. Start at home. Tell your spouse and children on a regular basis that you believe in them, that you think they are wonderful, that you love them, and that you are proud of them. David McClelland of Harvard found that the very best and happiest families, the families that produced the highest achieving children, were characterized as "positive expectations" families.

The parents continually fed their children a stream of positive messages, reaffirming how much they loved them and believed in them. No matter what happened in the short term, the children always knew that their parents were behind them 100 percent. And they didn't disappoint their parents.

3. Practice these same behaviors with your staff and coworkers. The very best managers, entrepreneurs, and salespeople are "positive expectations" people, with everyone and in everything they do.

4. Expect the best of yourself. Imagine that you have unlimited potential and that you can accomplish anything that you put your mind to. Imagine that your future is limited only by your own imagination and that whatever you have accomplished up to now is only a small part of what you are truly capable of achieving. Imagine that your greatest moments lie ahead and that everything that has happened to you up to now has merely been preparation for the great things that are yet to come.

4. The Law of Attraction

—⁓—

You are a living magnet; you invariably attract into your life the people, situations, and circumstances that are in harmony with your dominant thoughts.

This is one of the great laws that explains much of success and failure in one's business and personal life. It has been written about as far back as the ancient Egyptian mystery schools, 3,000 years before Christ. It is so powerful, pervasive, and all-encompassing that it affects everything you do or say, or even think or feel.

Everything you have in your life, you have attracted to yourself because of the way you think, because of the person you are. You can change your life because you can change the way you think. You can change the person you are.

You have heard it said, "Birds of a feather flock together." "Like attracts like." "Whatever you want, wants you." These are ways of expressing the Law of Attraction.

Your thoughts are extremely powerful. They are like a form of mental energy that travels at the speed of light. They are so fine that they can go through any barrier. This is why, for example, you can think about a person, sometimes at a great distance, and in the next moment, the phone will ring and that person will be on the line. Your thoughts have connected with that person the moment you thought them.

Companies develop products, processes, services, and ways of doing business that attract an entire constellation of customers, employees, suppliers, financiers, and circumstances that are in harmony with the dominant thinking of the organization. It is as though every human ingredient inside and outside the organization is a musical instrument of some kind. Together, they make up a great symphony orchestra. They are all playing together and creating a form of music that constitutes the activities of your business and your life.

Whenever things are not going well in any organization, the fastest way to bring about change is to bring in a new person who changes the way people think and feel about themselves and what they are doing. New values, new visions, new strategies, and new policies toward customers and toward each other bring about rapid and often dramatic change.

How you can apply this law immediately:

1. Engage in a rigorous process of self-analysis, self-examination. Look closely at the world around you and see how it harmonizes with your thinking. Take full credit for all the good things in your life. They are there because you have attracted them to yourself. Then, look around you at the things you don't like and take full responsibility for them, as well. They are there because of you, because of some flaw in your thinking. What is that flaw, and what are you going to do about it?

2. Look into yourself and ask, What is it *in me* that is causing this situation? Assume as a basic principle that you are the ongoing architect of your own life, your own destiny. You continually create what happens to you by the way you think. What changes do you need to make in your thinking if you want to change or improve some aspect of your life?

5. The Law of Correspondence

—ᨑ—

Your outer world is a reflection of your inner world; it corresponds with your dominant patterns of thinking.

This is an extraordinary principle. It explains most happiness and unhappiness, most success and failure, most greatness and meanness in life. After years of study in this area, I still stand in awe before this powerful law, like standing and looking out over the vastness of the Grand Canyon.

Just think! Your outer world reflects your inner world in every way. Nothing can happen to or for you in the long term until it corresponds to something inside of you. If you want to change or improve anything in your life, you must begin by changing the inner aspects of your mind.

Sometimes this correspondence is called the "mental equivalent." Your greatest responsibility in life is to create within yourself the mental equivalent of what you want to experience on the outside. The fact is that you cannot achieve a goal on the outside until you have first created it on the inside.

It is as though your life is a 360-degree mirror. Wherever you look, there you are. Your relationships, for example, always reflect back to you the kind of person you are on the inside. Your attitude, your health, and your material conditions are a reflection of the way you think most of the time.

This is hard for most people to accept. Most people think that the problems in their lives are caused by other people and external circumstances. They are shocked and angered to be told that they are the primary architects of everything that happens to them. They want others to change. They want the world to change. But they do not want to change themselves.

The Law of Correspondence is a foundation principle of virtually all religions and schools of thought. It is really great news. It is the key to personal freedom and happiness. It is the high road to great success and fulfillment.

You can control only one thing in the world, and that is the way you think. However, when you take complete control over your thinking, you take control over all the other aspects of your life. By thinking and talking only about what you want, and by refusing to think or talk about what you don't want, you become the architect of your own destiny.

How you can apply this law immediately:

1. Look around you for examples of where your outer world of experience is a reflection of your inner world of thought, emo-

tion, and belief. How does your current situation in your business or career reflect your innermost attitudes and convictions toward your company, your coworkers, your products and services, your customers, and your goals? Be honest.

2. Begin today to build the consciousness, the mental equivalent, on the inside of the life you want to enjoy on the outside. Visualize and imagine that your business and career were perfect in every respect. What changes do you need to make in your thinking to create your inner world in such a way that it is consistent with what you want to experience on the outside?

Summary

All the business laws you will learn in this book are logical extensions of the Law of Cause and Effect, combined with the Laws of Belief, Expectations, Attraction, and Correspondence. They contain a single message: If you change the quality of your thinking, you change the quality of your life.

And since there is no limit to how much better you can think, there is no real limit to how much better your life can be. It's totally up to you.

CHAPTER TWO

The Laws of Success
—⚬⚬—

6. The Law of Control

7. The Law of Accident

8. The Law of Responsibility

9. The Law of Direction

10. The Law of Compensation

11. The Law of Service

12. The Law of Applied Effort

13. The Law of Overcompensation

14. The Law of Preparation

15. The Law of Forced Efficiency

16. The Law of Decision

17. The Law of Creativity

18. The Law of Flexibility

19. The Law of Persistence

The Laws of Success

—ɯɯ—

What is success? Success can be defined as "being happy with what you've got." Success is not necessarily determined by material possessions or accomplishments. You can enjoy success simply by reaching the point where you are perfectly content with your life in every respect and you feel no dissatisfaction or pressing need for anything else. In this sense, you can be a success sitting by yourself in a quiet place contemplating the world.

Achievement is different from success. Achievement refers to "getting what you want." Achievement requires the ability to set goals and objectives, to make plans of action, and then to implement those plans. Achievement requires that you overcome obstacles and difficulties in reaching the goals that you have set for yourself.

In both cases, success and achievement, the starting point of great accomplishment is for you to decide exactly what you want in every part of your personal and business life. Motivation requires "motive," and the clearer you are about your true motives, the more you will achieve and the faster you will achieve it.

The basic principle of human action is that everything you do is aimed at improving your life in some way. Every action of yours is guided by a purpose of some kind, whether clear or unclear. As Aristotle wrote, all behavior is "teleological" or purposeful—aimed at a goal. And the one factor that governs each of your actions is your desire to be better off than you would be in the absence of your action.

The remarkable truth is that you always seem to achieve the goals that you set for yourself. If your goal is a small one, for example, to get home at night and watch television, you will certainly achieve it. If your goal is a large one—to achieve financial success, prosperity, and prestige among the people you live and work with—you will achieve that as well.

Your mind contains a cybernetic, goal-seeking mechanism. Once you have programmed a target or a desire into your subconscious mind, your subconscious and your superconscious minds take on a power of their own that seems to both drive and steer you inevitably toward the attainment of your goal, whatever it is.

In this sense, goal achieving seems to happen almost automatically. This goal-seeking capacity is as natural to you as breathing in and breathing out. The difficulty always lies in your ability to set clear goals in the first place. When you learn and practice this critical skill, you will begin to achieve at a higher level almost immediately. You will begin to achieve your goals faster and with greater predictability.

The key to activating the Laws of Success is for you to become perfectly clear about what it is you want and exactly what it will look like when you have achieved it. Just as you wouldn't attempt to build a house without a plan, you wouldn't think of building a great life without a clear list of the goals you wish to attain and a written plan of action for the attainment of each of those goals.

Unfortunately, according to virtually every study, less than 3 percent of adults have clear, written goals and detailed plans to achieve them. According to Mark McCormack in his book *What They Still Don't Teach You at Harvard Business School*, this top 3 percent of goal setters are earning, on average, ten times as much in the same period as those people with no written goals at all.

You can move yourself into the top rank of people living today by the simple act of sitting down with a pad of paper and a pen and making a list of the things you want. Most people have never *how can you possibly know ... what you want ... every idea in your head ... of which would do in a pinch but ... you want ...*

THE LAWS OF SUCCESS   31

done this. The very act of writing out a description of what you want to accomplish and what you intend to do to accomplish it over the next three to five years will change your life.

When you write down your goals, you immediately become a different person. Your attitude toward yourself and your future changes in a very positive way. You feel more confident and optimistic. You feel more in control and in command of your life. Best of all, when your goals and plans are in writing, the probability of your accomplishing them increases ten times, or by about 1,000 percent.

A Simple Exercise to Change Your Life

Here is a simple but powerful exercise. Take out a piece of paper and make a list of ten goals that you want to achieve over the next twelve months. Write out these goals in the present tense, as though a year has passed and you have already achieved them.

Use the word "I" before each goal to personalize it, as in "I earn X number of dollars per year." "I achieve such and such level of sales (or profits)." Your subconscious mind accepts only commands that are personal, positive, and in the present tense.

This is an amazing exercise, almost magical. If all you do is write down ten goals on a sheet of paper and then put it away for a year, at the end of twelve months, when you take it out, you will be astonished. When you reread the list after one year, you will find that eight of your ten goals have been achieved, sometimes in the most remarkable of ways. Often your goals will materialize much faster.

An insurance executive from Houston took this recommendation from me at a seminar in Phoenix on a Saturday morning. That afternoon on the flight home, he made a list of ten things he wanted to accomplish within the next twelve months.

The following evening, Sunday, he reviewed the list and found, to his astonishment, that he had already accomplished five of his ten one-year goals. He quickly wrote down five more goals, bringing his list back up to ten. By the following Thursday evening, he had accomplished five more of the goals on his new list. He wrote and told me that he had achieved more in five days with written goals than he had expected to accomplish in an entire year of hard work.

The following laws of success will work for you when you work with them. They are universal principles that have been discovered, tested, and proven over the centuries. When you begin to apply them to your business and your life, you will be amazed at the things you accomplish and how much easier you accomplish them.

6. The Law of Control

—⁓—

You feel good about yourself to the degree
to which you feel that you are in control of
your own life.

The reverse of this law, of course, is that you feel negative about yourself to the degree to which you feel you are *not* in control of your own life or that you are controlled by other people or circumstances.

The psychological profession has long recognized the importance of feelings of control as a critical element in human personality and performance. The term that psychologists use is "locus of control." The locus, or place, of control refers to wherever you feel the control is located in any part of your life. If you feel that

you personally make the decisions that determine the c
your life, you are considered to have an "internal locus ᴏ⸗ ⸗⸗

If you feel that your boss, your bills, your childhood experiences, your health, or anything else controls you or forces you to
do or refrain from doing what you really want, you are considered
to have an "external locus of control."

The location of this place of control in your thinking is the
critical element in determining your personal level of health and
well-being. People with an *internal* locus of control, those who feel
that they are behind the wheels of their own lives, tend to be low-
stress, high-performance personalities. People with an *external*
locus of control, those who feel that what they are doing is dic-
tated by other people and pressures, tend to be high-stress, low-
performance personalities.

The field of cognitive psychology is focused on studying how
you think and the relationship of your thinking to your health and
happiness. More than twenty-five years of research in this field has
concluded that a "sense of control" is absolutely essential for you
to perform at your best.

The first corollary of the Law of Control is
Change is inevitable.

It is not only inevitable; it is also unavoidable. It is accelerating. It is unpredictable and discontinuous. It is affecting every
aspect of our lives.

Change is also scary for most people. There is a deep-rooted
desire on the part of most people to avoid change of any kind, even
positive change. This is why goals are so important. Goals allow
you to control the direction of change. Goals assure that change
in your life is predominantly in the direction that you want to go.
Goals give you control over the critical elements of your life. Goals
give you a greater sense of personal power and well-being.

The second corollary of the Law of Control is
Controlled change leads inevitably to greater
achievement than uncontrolled change.

By working every day toward the accomplishment of your most important goals, you virtually guarantee that you will feel better and accomplish more than if you didn't. You automatically exert a greater sense of control.

The third corollary of this law is
To take control of your life, you must begin by taking control of your mind.

Your ability to think the thoughts you want, and to determine the goals and results you desire, is the starting point of all happiness and high attainment. Successful, happy people make a habit of thinking and talking *only* about the things they want. Unsuccessful, unhappy people, unfortunately, spend most of their time thinking and talking about what they *don't* want. Because of the Laws of Belief, Expectations, Attraction, and Correspondence, whatever you think and talk about most of the time is going to appear in your life.

How you can apply this law immediately:

1. Examine your life carefully and notice the parts of your life that cause you the greatest amounts of stress, anger, or frustration on a regular basis. These are usually situations in which you feel you have little or no control. The starting point of dealing with a stressful person or situation is for you to identify it clearly.

2. Resolve to make a decision in each of these areas, to either get in or get out, to do something or to stop whatever you are doing. Whether it is a job, a relationship, or an investment of time, money, or emotion, the act of making a decision to take

an action of some kind will reduce your stress and increase your feeling of personal power almost immediately.

Remember always that you are where you are and what you are because of yourself, because of your own choices and decisions. If you are not happy with your situation, it is up to you to make different and better choices and decisions. And you are always free to choose.

7. The Law of Accident

—m—

Life is a series of random occurrences and
things just happen by accident.

This law is really a psychological principle that is accepted without question by most people, thereby making it a law for them. If you believe something to be true, even if it is completely false, you will think and feel in such a way that it will be true for you.

The first corollary of this law is
By failing to plan, you are planning to fail.

No one actually plans deliberately to fail. No one decides in advance to live a life of underachievement and frustration, but by failing to decide exactly what you want, you end up living unconsciously and unintentionally by the Law of Accident. Then, what happens to you in life will appear to be a series of random occurrences over which you have little control.

People who live by the Law of Accident say things like "You can't fight city hall." "It's not what you know, it's who you know." "Success is just a matter of being in the right place at the right time." These people usually believe that success is largely due to luck and circumstances and that it has very little to do with themselves. They are living by the Law of Accident.

To show how prevalent this attitude is, in a recent survey, 63 percent of respondents said that they believed that the only way they were going to be able to retire financially independent was if they won a lottery of some kind. This means that the majority of people think that their financial lives are simply a great gamble in which they exert very little control. They are living by accident.

A well-known national politician, a member of Congress, said recently, referring to successful people in general, "Those who have done well at the gaming table of life should be forced to share their winnings with those who have not been so fortunate." This kind of thinking encourages more and more people to believe that life is just a game of chance. They live by the Law of Accident, believing that they are victims of circumstance and that there is nothing they can do to help themselves.

People who live by the Law of Accident tend to be negative, pessimistic, and helpless and feel as though they have little control over their lives.

People living under the shadow of the Law of Accident blame others for their problems. They continually make excuses, perform well below their potentials, and indulge in various forms of escapism, such as endless television watching, alcohol, drugs, and aimless socializing.

The wonderful thing about goals is that the very act of setting goals frees you from living under the Law of Accident and puts you squarely under the Law of Control and the Law of Cause and Effect. The setting of goals gives you a feeling of power, purpose, and forward direction. Goal setting puts you in charge of your life and makes you feel terrific about yourself.

This is why goal setting is called the "master skill" of success. It is the one skill that is probably more important to your overall happiness and well-being than any other skill that you can develop. It puts you in the driver's seat.

How you can apply this law immediately:

1. Identify the areas of your business life where you feel dissatisfied and you feel that there is nothing you can do about it. What one change could you make that would put you back in control? Whatever your answer, resolve to do something about it today.

2. Take action immediately to assert control over the situations in your life that are causing you to feel trapped and frustrated. If you could wave a magic wand and have complete power to change any condition or situation in your life, what would it be and what would you change?

8. The Law of Responsibility
—⁙—

You are completely responsible for
everything you are and for everything you
become and achieve.

You become what you think about most of the time. And only you can decide what you think and how you think about it. Therefore, only you are responsible for what happens in your life. From the age of eighteen onward, sometimes earlier, you make your own choices and decisions. You are then responsible for the results of those choices and decisions.

You are where you are and what you are because of yourself—no one else. You are doing the work you have chosen to do and earning the amount you have chosen to earn. You are always free to choose, but once you have chosen, or failed to choose, you must accept the consequences of your choices.

The concept of individual responsibility is a major issue in life and society, perhaps the most important issue of all. There are basically two schools of thought on this issue. On the one side are those who believe that no one is really responsible for anything. They believe that the government or society or business is to blame for anything unfortunate that happens to anyone, anywhere.

The other school of thought says that in a society of individual freedom, individual responsibility is absolute. It is essential and unavoidable. This group says that people are responsible for the consequences of their behavior. Individuals are responsible for the things they do and for the things they neglect to do.

The fact about responsibility is that for you to be free and happy, it is not optional. It is mandatory. Greater progress in your life is possible only to the degree to which you accept a higher level of responsibility in that area. No one else can or will do it for you.

The interesting thing about responsibility is that the more of it you accept and the more you look to yourself, the more other people will want to help you. But the less responsibility you accept and the more you blame others, the smaller is the number of people who will want to have anything to do with you.

The first corollary of the Law of Responsibility is
You are always free to choose what you think and
what you do.

Wherever you are or whatever you are doing, it is largely a result of your own choices. Therefore, you are where you are and what you are because of your own conduct and your own behavior. Like it or not, you have chosen to be there.

Because you have freedom of choice and you can do and say what you want, you can never evade responsibility for the things that you do or fail to do, for the things you say or fail to say.

The second corollary of this law is
Responsibility begins with your taking full and complete control over the content of your conscious mind.

It is what you think and how you think about it that determines your reality. And since only you can control what you think, the very act of taking control of your thoughts and keeping them focused only on what you want (and away from the things you don't want) is the beginning of self-mastery, self-control, and personal power.

The third corollary of the Law of Responsibility is
No one is coming to the rescue.

If it is to be, it is up to you. If you want your life to get better, you must get better. If you want things to change, you must change. If you want things to improve, you must first improve yourself.

The most wonderful reward you receive from accepting complete responsibility is the tremendous sense of control and freedom you experience as a result. The acceptance of complete responsibility makes you feel positive and happy about yourself. It frees you completely from the Law of Accident. It puts you on to the high road to great achievement. It enables you to put your foot on the accelerator of your own potential and move more rapidly toward the accomplishment of more of the things that are important to you.

How to apply this law immediately:

1. Take responsibility for your work, for every aspect of your job. The top people in every industry act as if they own the place. They see themselves as self-employed, no matter who signs their paychecks. And they are always the most appreciated and respected people in the company.

   Never make excuses or blame anyone else for anything. Never say or even think, "That's not my job!" This is the way people who have no future think and talk. This is not for you. You are responsible.

2. Volunteer for assignments, for additional work. Be the first person to raise your hand at a meeting when something needs to be done. Take initiative. Be proactive. Go to your boss and tell him or her that you want more responsibility. And keep asking for it, again and again.

   When you get an assignment or you volunteer for something that needs to be done, do it quickly and well. Develop a sense of urgency. Treat every opportunity to perform as though it were a fumble in a football game and you have a chance to score the winning touchdown. Grab it and run with it.

9. The Law of Direction

—⚹—

Successful people have a clear sense of
purpose and direction in every area of their
lives.

Lloyd Conant, founder of Nightingale Conant Corporation of Chicago, the biggest producer and distributor of audio programs on success and achievement in the world, worked with and stud-

ied successful people for more than fifty years. He came to the conclusion that **"Success is goals, and all else is commentary."**

Your ability to set clear, specific goals for yourself in every area
of your life will do more to guarantee you higher levels of success
and achievement than any other single skill or quality. Absolute
clarity about what you want is the starting point of all great accomplishment.

The more definite and focused you are, the easier it is for you
to make better decisions on your priorities and the use of your
time. The more time you spend on your most important goals, the
more you accomplish, and the better you get at accomplishing
even more. And the more you achieve, the better you feel about
yourself, the more you feel like a winner and the more you want
to achieve. You put yourself onto an upward spiral that leads to
ever-greater accomplishments. You feel terrific about yourself.

How to apply this law immediately:

1. Take out a sheet of paper and write the words "Dream List" at
   the top of the page, along with today's date. You might want
   to use a spiral notebook for this exercise so that you have several pages together in the same place.

   Create your own "five-year fantasy." Imagine that five years
   have passed and your life is now perfect in every respect.
   Imagine that all your goals have been achieved, all your problems have been solved, and you are living the life of your dreams.

   Imagine that your income, bank account, relationships,
   family life, health, work, and career are ideal in every way.
   What would they look like? What would you be doing? Who
   would you be with? Who would you no longer be with? How
   much would you be earning? What sort of lifestyle and family
   would you have? What kind of home, car, clothes, and level of
   physical fitness would you have?

Describe your future vision for yourself in complete detail by writing out everything you could ever imagine wanting to have on your Dream List.

Some people will come up with a list of only five or ten items. Others will come up with a list of 200 or 300 items that they would like to accomplish in the next five years.

For there to be motivation, there must be a motive. Fully 85 percent of your motivation is determined by the consequences that you anticipate, or the things that you hope to achieve, as a result of what you do. The more clear you are about what you want, the more motivated and determined you will be to accomplish it.

Once you've written down a list of your dreams and goals, a list of everything that you would like to have in your life, the next step is for you to assign priorities to them.

Next to the items that are most important to you, the ones that can make the greatest difference in your life and that you desire most intensely, write the letter "A."

Next to the items that you would like to have but are not as important or as life changing as those in the first category, write the letter "B." Next to each of the remaining items, goals that you wrote down that you would like but you don't care about passionately, write the letter "C."

Now, transfer all of your A goals to a separate sheet of paper. Then ask yourself, What one goal on this list, if I were to achieve it, would have the greatest positive impact on my life?

Write "A-1" next to this primary goal. Then ask yourself, If I could achieve only one more goal on this list, which one would it be?

Write "A-2" next to your second most important goal. Go through the entire list of A goals with the same question, writing "A-3," "A-4," and so on until you have organized all of your A goals in order of priority.

Your A-1 goal should be your "major definite purpose," the most important goal in your life. The accomplishment of this goal will lead you to the accomplishment of more of your other goals than any other single goal on your list. Your selection of an A-1 major definite purpose, your most important goal, is your starting point to personal greatness. By deciding on this goal for yourself, you join the top 3 percent of high-achieving men and women in our society.

In our strategic planning sessions with corporations, we use a similar exercise. We ask the executives in the session to imagine that five years have passed and the company is perfect in every respect. We go around the room and invite each person to describe the company from his or her point of view, from his or her particular position of responsibility.

We then discuss and agree upon the most important goals that the company would have achieved if it were ideal in every way. The main goal or output for the company soon becomes clear. It then becomes obvious that most of the other goals are inputs, or steps toward the achievement of the main goal.

For example, in strategic planning with a large national restaurant chain, we came up with several goals having to do with increased volume per unit; food quality; reputation in the marketplace; hiring, training, and promotion strategies; service standards; internal financial controls; and so on. However, the major definite purpose agreed upon was increasing the share price by 300 percent over the next five years.

It became immediately apparent that the other goals were subgoals that would need to be achieved if the company were to be profitable enough to realize its goal of a tripled share price. The other goals were the inputs, the accomplishments of which would lead to the desired output.

In reviewing your personal goals, you should divide them into three categories. The first category is your personal and family goals. These are qualitative goals, having to do with people, time, and quality of life.

These are the reasons "why" you are doing what you are doing. You should be crystal clear about the underlying reasons why you want the material and tangible goals that you are working for. Many people get sidetracked working for material things and lose all sight of the reasons why they are doing it.

Your second set of goals is your career and material goals. These are the "what" of your goal list. These are the goals that you have to reach in order to get to the "why." The "what," or business and financial goals on your list, will be career achievements, financial income, and sales or profits, the money and material objects of your life.

The third type of goals is your personal and professional development goals. These are the "how" goals. These are the tasks that you must do, or become competent at doing, in order to achieve the material goals that will lead you to the accomplishment of your personal and family goals.

You need goals in each of these three areas for your life to be in balance and for you to perform at your very best.

2. Make detailed plans of action to achieve your goals. Once you have set priorities on your original list of goals, divided them into As, Bs, and Cs, and then transferred your As on to a single page and organized them in order of priority, you are ready to begin the planning stage. In the planning stage, take a clean sheet of paper and write your A-1 goal at the top of the page in the present tense, as though it were already a reality.

For example, you could write, "I earn $100,000 per year." Then make a list of everything you can think of that you can do to achieve that goal. As time passes, you will think of additional actions you can take, which you should add to your list. Keep adding new ideas until your list is complete.

Do the same for each of your other A goals. At the end of this process, you will have a list of A goals, each accompanied by a list of several ideas to accomplish each one.

Then organize each list of activities by time and priority. Which are the tasks that you can or should do or begin first? What are the actions that are most important and would make the greatest difference in the attainment of the goal? Write down an A, B, or C next to each of the items and then write down A-1, A-2, A-3, B-1, B-2, B-3, and so on next to each item.

You will now have a list of your most important goals, organized by priority. You will have a list of the activities you must engage in to achieve those goals, also organized by priority. You will have a goal and a plan for each important area of your life.

Review this plan each day, morning and evening. Resolve to do something every day to move yourself toward the attainment of one or more of your most important goals. This daily work on your goals enables you to develop and maintain a certain degree of momentum. With this momentum, you will be astonished at how rapidly you begin to make progress on even your largest and most challenging goals.

In brief, here is a simple, powerful, and proven method for setting and achieving any goal. Practice it yourself and teach it to others:

Step one: Decide *exactly* what you want. Most people never do this.

Step two: *Write it down* in clear, specific, detailed language.

Step three: *Set a deadline.* Set subdeadlines if the goal is large, long term, or complicated.

Step four: *Make a list* of everything you can think of doing to achieve your goal.

Step five: *Organize your list into a plan* based on priorities and sequence, based on what comes first and then what must be done before something else can be done.

Step six: *Take action* on your plan immediately. Don't delay.

Step seven: *Do something every day,* no matter how small, that moves you toward your goal.

The Key to Great Success

After a seminar in Minneapolis recently, a businessman told me a great story. He said that he had come to a seminar of mine with a friend about eight years ago. He was from a farm family and lived in a small town outside of Minneapolis. He had never heard about goal setting before.

He told me that he returned home that night, wrote down his goals, made a plan, and took immediate action. From that day to this, he told me, he had disciplined himself to do something every single day that moved him toward his major goal, whatever it happened to be at the time. He said that his income had increased just over 1,000 percent, ten times, in eight years. He concluded his story by telling me that it was the idea of "doing something every day" that was more important than anything else he had ever learned.

When you begin to practice regular, systematic, daily goal setting and planning, combined with the other principles you learn in this book, you will get results that will amaze you, and all the people around you. You will accomplish more in a year or two than others accomplish in five or ten years.

10. The Law of Compensation

—∞—

You are always fully compensated for
whatever you do, positive or negative.

There is perfect justice in the world, at least in the long term. Whatever you put in, you get out. The more you give, the more you receive. If you want to increase the quality and quantity of your rewards, you must increase the quality and quantity of your contribution.

My friend Zig Ziglar, the speaker and motivator, has formulated what we might call Ziglar's Law, which is a paraphrase of the Law of Compensation. It says, "You can have anything you want in life if you just help enough other people get what they want."

The Law of Compensation is a restatement of the Law of Cause and Effect, or the Law of Sowing and Reaping, which says, "Whatsoever a man soweth, that also shall he reap."

The significance of this law is that you cannot reap something unless you have first sown something. Put another way, whatever you are reaping today is a measure of what you have sown in the past. If you want to reap something more or different in the future, you have to sow something more or different or better in the present.

In Ralph Waldo Emerson's essay *Compensation*, he says, "The longer you put in without getting out, the greater will be your return when it finally comes."

This law or principle runs throughout all of human experience and explains much of success and failure, happiness and unhappiness. This is the basic principle of all business activities, to produce products and services that people want and will buy in sufficient quantities to compensate for the cost of bringing them to the market in the first place.

Successful individuals and organizations are continually looking for ways to improve the quality and quantity of their offerings. They continually seek ways to add value, to serve their customers better than anyone else. So should you. Put yourself on the side of the angels by always asking, What can I do to increase the value of my services to my customers today?

How to apply this law immediately:

1. Decide what it is that you really want and then determine the price you will have to pay to achieve it. For everything you want in life, there is a price you must pay, in full and in advance.

2. Decide upon the new skills and qualities you will need to accomplish your goals. Remember, to achieve something you have never achieved before, you must do something you have never done before. You must become someone you have never been before. Whatever you want, you will have to pay a price measured in terms of sacrifice, time, effort, and personal discipline. Decide what it is and start paying that price today.

11. The Law of Service

—ɷ—

Your rewards in life will be in direct proportion to the value of your service to others.

We all make our livings and add meaning to our lives by serving other people in some way. We are all dependent upon thousands and millions of other people for the food we eat, the clothes we wear, the homes we live in, and the various elements that make our lives enjoyable and worthwhile. Our primary job as members of society is to find the best way to incorporate ourselves into the fabric of society by serving as many others as well as we possibly can.

The first corollary of this law is
All fortunes begin with the sale of personal services.

There are almost five million self-made millionaires in America, including many people from the most difficult backgrounds imaginable. In addition, there are countless immigrants who have become financially independent who arrived in the United States with no money, no language skills, limited education, and no friends or contacts. Each of these people passed the magic million-dollar mark in personal worth by finding a way to serve others more effectively. And so can you.

The second corollary of the Law of Service is
If you wish to increase the quantity of your rewards, you must first increase the quality and quantity of your service.

The more you put in, the more you will get out. According to every study, the highest paid Americans—entrepreneurs, executives, professionals, salespeople—work an average of fifty-nine hours per week, for many years, to become successful. They become increasingly more productive and valuable to their customers until they finally make it. Then everyone tells them how "lucky" they are.

The third corollary of the Law of Service is
Everyone works on commission.

Everyone is paid "a piece of the action," a share of the income or profit from the economic activity of the organization. No matter how your compensation is structured or how it is described, it is ultimately based on the value of your service, the size of your contribution.

To put it another way, you are ultimately paid for results. The good news is that you can increase your value, and ultimately the amount you earn, by increasing the quality and quantity of your results. And in the long run, there is no other way.

This focus on results, on pleasing customers better than your competitors, is the guiding force of successful businesses. The top managers in the leading companies all seem to have an "obsession with customer service."

The most successful men and women in our society are those who are able to "lose themselves" in serving the people who depend upon them, their customers, their employers and others, for what they do.

When you combine the Law of Compensation with the Law of Service, you have the keys to obtaining anything that you really want in life. You get out exactly what you put in, and wonderfully enough, you have complete control over what you put in. No one can ever stop you from putting in more every single day. No one can ever stop you from going the extra mile, from always doing more than you're paid for.

When you devote yourself completely to serving your customers—your boss, your staff, the people who purchase or use your products and services—you start to enjoy a wonderful feeling of meaning and purpose. You feel that you are really making a difference in the world. When you know that you are putting in more than you are taking out, that you are making a real contribution, you feel terrific about yourself.

When you throw your whole heart into making your customers happy and serving them better than anyone else, you take complete control over your future. You put your career and your financial life onto the fast track.

How you can apply this law immediately:

1. Become crystal clear about who your customers really are. Your customers include everyone whom you depend upon for any of the things you want in your business and personal life. Your customers also include all those who are dependent on you for their success or satisfaction.

   Your internal customers at work are your boss, your co-workers, and your staff. These people are dependent on you in many ways. What do they need from you to perform at their best? How could you become more valuable to them?

2. Determine your most important external customers, the people outside your organization whom you must satisfy if you want them to continue doing business with you. Who are your most important customers, both the customers of today and the customers of the future? What could you do to increase the value of your service to the people who are instrumental to the survival of your business?

   Who are the people in your personal life who depend on you in some way: your family, your friends, the people in your community? How could you serve them better? What could you do to enhance or enrich their lives?

   Whatever your answers to these questions, write them down, make a plan, and then take action. Your whole future depends upon it.

12. The Law of Applied Effort

—ᴍ—

All worthwhile achievements are amenable
to hard work.

Nothing will bring you to the attention of your superiors faster
than your developing a reputation for being a hard worker. People
who are in a position to help you advance in your career will always
be impressed by your willingness to work harder and longer than
anyone else.

In Dr. Thomas Stanley's study of affluent Americans, *The
Millionaire Next Door*, he reports that almost every one of the
self-made millionaires he interviewed told him that their success was due more to hard work than to any other factor. In
America, you work forty hours per week for survival. If all you
work is forty hours, all you earn is enough to survive. You tread
water and you basically stay even. But you don't get very far
ahead and you never achieve the kind of success that is possible
for you.

Every hour you put in over forty, either on your job or on
yourself, improving your knowledge and skills, is an investment
in your success, in your future. You can tell where you are going
to be in three to five years with unerring accuracy by simply
looking at the number of hours over forty that you are working
each week.

The average workweek for both executives and small-business
owners in America is approximately fifty-eight to fifty-nine
hours. Many successful men and women work seventy and eighty
hours per week during the critical formative stages of their
careers.

The first corollary of the Law of Applied Effort is

All great success is preceded by a long period of
hard, hard work in a single direction toward a clearly
defined purpose.

You must continually ask yourself, What am I trying to do?
and How am I trying to do it? It's not enough just to work hard
or to work long hours. You must be working on high-value tasks
and activities aimed toward the accomplishment of meaningful
and important goals.

The second corollary of this law is

The harder you work, the luckier you get.

It seems that your ability to work very, very hard will open up
the doors of opportunity for you and will bring to your assistance
all manner of people and resources that you could not have imagined would come your way. Your commitment to hard work creates a force field of positive energy around you that attracts positive people and greater opportunities into your life.

The third corollary of the Law of Applied Effort is

To achieve more than the average person, you must
work longer and harder than the average person.

This is simply a way of restating the fact that you can get more
out of life only if you put more into life. And the more you put in,
the more you will get out. The Law of Cause and Effect is absolute.
You will invariably reap what you sow, and if you sow more, you
will eventually reap more.

How you can apply this law immediately:

1. Resolve today that from now on you are going to work longer
   and harder than anyone else. How could you organize your life
   so you could start a little earlier, work a little harder, and stay

a little later? For example, by starting just one hour before the others, working at lunchtime, and staying one hour later, you can carve out three extra hours of productive time each day.

One hour of focused, uninterrupted work time will give you the equivalent of two to three hours of normal, interrupted working time during the day. Your productivity will double and so will your value. And by coming in a little earlier and staying a little later, you will avoid most of the traffic!

2. Begin today to organize your days and your weeks so that you put in forty-five, fifty, or even sixty hours per week. You will be amazed at how easy it is to create this extra time, and you will very quickly come to the attention of the people who can help you get ahead, without your having to say a word.

More than anything, *work all the time you work!* Don't waste time in idle chatting with coworkers, personal telephone calls, long coffee breaks, and extended lunch hours. When you work, work! Put your head down and make every minute count. When you come in early or stay late, get right to work, without delay. Work on high-value tasks. Avoid time-wasting conversations. Socialize on your own time. Remember, people are watching.

13. The Law of Overcompensation

—⁓—

*If you always do more than you are paid for,
you will always be paid more than you are
getting now.*

To be a big success, you must always be looking for opportunities to go beyond the requirements of your job. Napoleon Hill, perhaps the foremost researcher on success in the first half of the twentieth century, concluded that one of the keys to great success in America was the willingness to "go the extra mile."

Because of this principle, your future is unlimited. There is no restriction on the extra things that you can do to add greater value to your work. You can go the extra mile in everything that you do, every day and in every way. You can always be looking for opportunities to exceed expectations.

Earl Nightingale advised that you should "Always do more than you're paid for or you'll never be paid much more than you're getting now." The only way that you can reap more is by sowing more. The only way that you can be paid more is by adding greater value to your work and by achieving more and better results.

A young woman who was working as a secretary for a large company in Florida came to me recently at a seminar and told me her story. She said she had listened to one of my audio programs, and as a result, she had set a goal to increase her income by 50 percent. In her heart, however, she didn't really believe it was possible because of the salary structure in her company.

Nonetheless, she began applying the Law of Overcompensation to her work. She started looking for ways to increase the value of her service to her boss, to do more than she was paid for. She applied the law to everything she did. She learned new skills on her own time. She began a little earlier and stayed a little later. She took on additional responsibilities and performed them to the best of her abilities.

She noticed the tasks that her boss didn't like to do and that took up a good deal of his time, such as replying to routine correspondence. One day, she wrote replies to several letters for him and then took them to him to review. He was both amazed and delighted. He began giving her more and more of his routine work, all of which she did quickly and well.

To make a long story short, she told me that over the next year, her boss gradually raised her salary, in three stages, from $1,500 per month to $1,750, to $2,000, and eventually to $2,250 per month, a 50 percent increase. And he gave her these increases without her ever having asked for them!

What she did each day was to seek out ways to work harder and smarter and to serve her boss better. He increased her pay because he recognized how much she had increased her value to him.

The remarkable thing is this: She had worked to the age of twenty-five to get her salary up to $1,500 per month. In just six months, by applying these principles, she increased her salary by fifty percent. And these principles can work for you as well. It is simply a matter of applying these laws to your work every day.

How you can apply this law immediately:

1. Think about your work. Where and in what way could you work better, smarter, more efficiently? What could you delegate, outsource, simplify, or eliminate so that you can have more time to do the few things you do that are the most important?

2. Identify the areas of your work where you could go the extra mile, where you could do more than anyone else expects. Where and in what way could you work harder, in a more disciplined way, to achieve even more of the most important results of your job?

   Go to your boss and ask him or her if there is any task that you could take off his or her hands. Look for ways to make your boss's life easier, and your boss will find ways to make your life better as well.

14. The Law of Preparation

—m—

Effective performance is preceded by painstaking preparation.

The mark of the serious person, or the real professional, in any field is that he takes far more time to prepare than the average. The nonserious person, or the nonprofessional, always attempts to bluff or to "wing it." He tries to get by with a minimum of preparation. He doesn't realize that his level of preparation is immediately evident to everyone around him.

A quote from Abraham Lincoln shaped my life and my attitude as I was growing up. He said, as a young man in Springfield, Illinois, "I shall study and prepare myself and some day my chance will come." He recognized, as do all great men and women, that painstaking preparation was the key to his future.

The first corollary of the Law of Preparation is

Do your homework; it is the details that trip you up every single time.

Great successes are often determined by attention to the smallest details. One fact, one inaccuracy, can make all the difference. And everything counts.

My friend Joel Weldon gave a wonderful talk a few years ago to the National Speakers Association, entitled "Elephants Don't Bite." The central message of his talk was that it was the "mosquitoes" of life, the small things that you tend to ignore, that cause you the most trouble. No one ever gets bitten by an elephant, but people get bitten by mosquitoes all the time. His message was simple: If you want to get to the top of your field, you must be fastidious about the little things because, as a minister once said, "the devil is in the details."

**The second corollary of the Law of Preparation
comes from business guru Peter Drucker, who wrote,**
"Action without thinking is the cause of every failure."

Taking action before thinking through the details and their possible consequences seems to be the underlying cause of most failure in life. The reverse of this statement, of course, is that action preceded by accurate thinking and thorough planning is the reason for virtually every success.

This doesn't mean that you will automatically be successful if you plan thoroughly in advance. But it does mean that you will almost always fail if you don't. Murphy's various laws of organization can be summarized in the following statement: "Whatever can go wrong, will go wrong. And of all the possible things that can go wrong, the worst possible thing will go wrong at the worst possible time and cost the greatest amount of money."

The first comment on Murphy's Law is that "Murphy was an optimist." Never assume or take anything important for granted. If it is important enough to matter, it is important enough to check and double-check.

How you can apply this law immediately:

1. Think through your most important tasks and responsibilities. Think on paper. Write down every detail of the matter and review your notes carefully.

2. Seek out the inputs and opinions of others before you make a major decision or commitment. Who else has dealt with a similar situation? What insights can he or she give you?

   Get the facts. Get the real facts, not the obvious facts, the apparent facts, the assumed facts, or the logical facts. Facts don't lie. Check and double-check. Your thinking and your decisions are only as good as the quality of the information you have to work with.

15. The Law of Forced Efficiency

—⚍—

The more things you have to do in a limited
period of time, the more you will be forced
to work on your most important tasks.

This is another way of saying that there is never enough time
to do everything, but there is always enough time to do the most
important things.

The more you take on, the more likely it is that you will be
forced to act with maximum efficiency. You will have to think,
analyze, and evaluate your tasks and activities more carefully. You
will be forced to spend your limited mental and physical energy
on just those tasks that are the most vital to your success.

The first corollary of the Law of Forced Efficiency is

There will never be enough time to do everything
that you have to do.

The busier and more successful you become, the more valid
this corollary will be for you. If you have ample time to do your
work, you are probably underemployed, underpaid, and moving
along the low road to underachievement and disappointment in
your career. If you are successful, you will almost always have too
much to do and too little time.

The second corollary of this law is

Only by stretching yourself can you discover how
much you are truly capable of.

You can discover how much you can do only by trying to do
too much. You can find out how far you can go only by going too
far. You learn your true capacity only by stretching yourself to your
limits.

For you to be truly happy, you must know that you are working at the outer edge of your potential. You need to feel fully challenged by your work. You need to do what you love, love what you do, and put your whole heart into your work.

The third corollary of this law is

You perform at your highest potential only when you are focusing on the most valuable use of your time.

This is the key to personal and business success. It is the central issue in personal efficiency and time management. You must always be asking yourself, What is the most valuable use of my time right now?

Discipline yourself to work exclusively on the one task that, at any given time, is the answer to this question. Keep yourself on track and focused on your most important responsibilities by asking yourself, over and over, What is the most valuable use of my time right now?

How you can apply this law immediately:

1. Remember that you can do only one thing at a time. Stop and think before you begin. Be sure that the task you do is the highest-value use of your time. Remind yourself that anything else you do while your most important task remains undone is a relative waste of time.

2. Be clear about the most valuable work that you do for your organization. Whatever it is, resolve to concentrate on doing that specific task before anything else.

   Why are you on the payroll? What specific, tangible, measurable results are expected of you? And of all the different results you are capable of achieving, which are the most important to your career at this moment? Whatever the answer, this is where you must focus your energies, and nowhere else.

16. The Law of Decision

—∿—

Every great leap forward in life is preceded by
a clear decision and a commitment to action.

All high-achieving men and women are decisive in their thinking and in their actions. They think things through carefully in
advance. They decide exactly what they want, and then they make
definite decisions. They then take specific actions to turn those
decisions into realities.

In your life, you have had experiences where you have been
unsure of what to do. You have gone back and forth and felt more
and more uncomfortable and distracted. You finally resolved your
dilemma by making a clear decision, one way or another. In looking back, you will probably find that that decision was the turning point for you in that situation, or perhaps even in your life.
Everything else flowed from your decision.

The ability to make good decisions is one of the most important skills of the successful person. In studies where the careers of
managers who were promoted rapidly were compared to those of
managers who were passed over for promotion, researchers found
that the one distinguishing behavior of the more rapidly promoted
managers is that they were more decisive in everything they did.

The interesting discovery that came out of these studies was
that when both groups of managers were given written tests with
hypothetical problems, both sets of managers were equally accurate in their *written* decisions. On the actual job, however, the
more successful managers were willing to actually make the decisions and take action while the unsuccessful managers were afraid
to decide for fear of making a mistake.

Developing the habit of decisiveness can be the critical factor that enables you to take command of a situation and puts you onto the fast track in your career.

I have spoken to countless men and women whose lives had changed for the better at a certain point. In almost every case, they told me that the change came when they finally decided to "get serious." They finally decided to quit sitting on the fence. They decided to make a specific decision of some kind and then throw their whole hearts into a particular course of action.

High achievers are not necessarily those who make the right decisions, but they are those people who make their decisions right. They accept feedback and self-correct. They take in new information and they change if necessary. But they are always decisive, always moving forward, never wishy-washy or vacillating in their attitudes and their approaches to life.

The first corollary of the Law of Decision is simply this:
Act boldly and unseen forces will come to your aid.

When you confront a situation boldly and step forward courageously, a series of unseen forces, most of which are explained by the laws in this book, seem to emerge to help you achieve your goals. Your willingness to take action rather than to delay or procrastinate seems to bring universal powers to your assistance.

The next corollary comes from the wonderful 1935 book by Dorothea Brande entitled *Wake Up and Live*. She writes about the discovery that changed her life and the lives of thousands of others who heard it from her in her public talks.

The second corollary of the Law of Decision is the simple success formula

Act as if it were impossible to fail, and it shall be.

This is one of the most powerful of all success principles. When you imagine that your success will be guaranteed if you will simply take action, and you act on that premise, a whole series of forces begins to support you and move you toward the attainment of your desires. When you are in doubt for any reason, act as if it were impossible to fail, and push forward.

The third corollary of the Law of Decision comes from the famous Nike commercial that says

"Just do it!"

These three words really summarize one of the great formulas for success. "Just do it!" Set your goals, make your plans, organize your priorities, imagine it is impossible to fail, and then, just do it!

How you can apply this law immediately:

1. Define the areas of your life and work where you need to make some clear, unequivocal decisions. Decide to "fish or cut bait!" Get in or get out. Remember that any decision is usually better than no decision at all.

   As William Shakespeare said in *Hamlet,* "Take arms against a sea of troubles, and in so doing, end them."

2. Be decisive. Go for it! Take a chance! Act boldly, and unseen forces will come to your aid. And do it now.

17. The Law of Creativity

—ɯ—

Every advance in human life begins with an
idea in the mind of a single person.

It is the ideas you generate, more than anything else, that will
enable you to solve your problems, overcome your obstacles, and
achieve your goals. Ideas are the keys to the future. It is not possible for you to achieve anything of value except to the degree to
which you think creatively and do something new and different
from what has been done before. All it takes is a small innovation
to lay the foundation for a fortune and launch you toward great
success.

The first corollary of this law is

Your ability to generate constructive ideas is, to all
intents and purposes, unlimited. Therefore, your
potential is unlimited as well.

Ideas are a mode of transportation, a vehicle that you can use
to take yourself from wherever you are to wherever you want to
go. Your job is to generate as many ideas as possible, evaluate them
carefully against your current goals, and then take action on them.
The greater the quantity of ideas that you develop, the greater will
be the quality of the ideas you have available to you.

There is virtually no obstacle in life that you cannot overcome
with the power of thought, with the power of concentration, with
the power of ideas.

The second corollary of this law comes from
Napoleon Hill who said,
Whatever the mind of man can conceive and
believe, it can achieve.

Your mind is designed in such a way that you cannot have an idea on the one hand without also having the ability to bring that idea into reality on the other. The very existence of an idea in your conscious mind means that you have within you and around you the capacity to turn it into reality. The only question you have to answer is, How badly do you want it?

The third corollary of creativity comes from
Napoleon Bonaparte who said,
Imagination rules the world.

Everything you see around you is the result of what was originally an idea in the mind of a single person. Our entire man-made world is the result of thought brought into reality.

The fourth corollary of this law comes from
Albert Einstein, who said,
Imagination is more important than facts.

There have been countless occasions in your life, and in the lives of others, where the facts say one thing but your ideas and creative ability have enabled you to do something completely different.

An idea or an insight at a critical moment can be the turning point in your life. All great changes in human life and destiny begin with an idea that enables you to see things differently and to take an action that you would not have taken in the absence of that idea.

Wherever you are, whatever you are doing, whatever your situation, you have the creative capacity, in the form of an infinite ability to generate ideas, to solve any problem and achieve any goal. There are virtually no limits to what you can accomplish except for the limits you place on your own imagination.

How you can apply this law immediately:

1. Practice the "Mindstorming" method of idea generation on every problem, question, or goal. More people have become wealthy and successful with this method of creative thinking than with any other. Here is how it works.

   Select any goal or problem you have and write it in the form of a question at the top of a sheet of paper. Then, write twenty answers to the question in the present tense, as though you are doing them already.

   For example, you could write, "What can I do to double my income over the next two or three years?" You could then answer, "I come to work one hour early every day and plan my day in advance." Discipline yourself to generate at least twenty answers in this way, and more if possible.

2. Select at least one idea or answer from your list and take action on it immediately. Your taking action keeps ideas coming all day long. It maintains your flow of creativity. And the more you practice this exercise, the more and better ideas you will generate. You will activate more of your brain. You will actually increase your intelligence.

   Do this exercise every day for a week, first thing in the morning, for whatever question or goal is most important to you at the moment. You will be amazed at the quality and quantity of ideas that spring from your imagination when you ask yourself the right questions and then write down the answers.

18. The Law of Flexibility

—∞—

Success is best achieved when you are clear
about the goal but flexible about the
process of getting there.

This is one of the most important discoveries made by high-
achieving men and women. When you set a clear goal for yourself
and make a plan, you usually have a fairly good idea of what it is
you will have to do to get whatever it is you want to achieve.
However, a thousand things can change, each of which can require
changes to your plan. The most optimistic and creative people are
those who are open, flexible, and fluid in the face of the inevitable
and continual changes they are required to make as they move
toward their goals.

The first corollary of the Law of Flexibility is
The continued experience of resistance and frustration is often an indication that you are doing the
wrong thing.

Whenever you feel that you are trying too hard and getting too
few results, be prepared to stand back and reexamine your plan.
Be sure that the goal that you are working toward is still the goal
that you desire. Consider the possibility that your chosen strategy
may be the wrong one for this situation. Be prepared to reconsider
and change your approach. Especially, get your ego out of the way.
Be more concerned with what is right than who is right.

Develop the mind-set of a computer programmer. When he
designs a computer program, he knows that the program will be
full of bugs when it is completed. No computer program ever
works perfectly the first time it is run. However, the programmer
accepts this as a fact of life and then begins to go back through the

program, line by line, to remove the defects. When the programmer is finished, the program will operate perfectly.

By the same token, whenever your plans do not seem to be bearing fruit, instead of pushing harder, stop and reevaluate the situation. Consider the possibility that you could be wrong in your present course of action. Revise your plans continually until they are faultless and they enable you to move forward smoothly, without anxiety or frustration.

The second corollary of this law is
You are only as free in life as the number of well-developed options you have available to you.

Your freedom and happiness are largely determined by the number of alternatives that you have developed in case your first choice doesn't work. The more thoroughly developed your options and alternatives, the more freedom you have. If one course of action doesn't develop as you expected, you will be fully prepared to switch to something else.

The very exercise of developing alternatives enables you to think more clearly. The more choices you have, the freer and more flexible you can be. The more choices you have, the more likely it is that one of them will work and enable you to achieve your goal.

The third corollary of the Law of Flexibility is
Crisis is change trying to take place.

Whenever you experience a crisis or roadblock of any kind, stand back for a moment and ask yourself, What change is trying to take place here? What is the message contained in this crisis?

You may be having a crisis in your work, in your personal relationships, with your health, or with your business. In almost every case, a crisis is an indication that something is definitely wrong and that pursuing the same course of action will only make it worse. What is the change that is trying to take place in your life right now?

The fourth corollary of the Law of Flexibility is

Errant assumptions lie at the root of every failure.

Almost every failure you experience will be because of an incorrect assumption that you have made and accepted without question. It is helpful for you to clarify and question your assumptions, especially when things are not going as well as you expected.

What are your assumptions? What are your explicit assumptions, the ones that you are clearly aware of? What are your implicit assumptions, the unconscious assumptions that you may be accepting without question?

What if your most cherished assumptions were wrong? What changes would you have to make? How would you change your course of action if something that you were assuming to be true turned out not to be true at all?

Whenever you make the right decisions and you achieve your goals on schedule, it is because the assumptions that you were operating on turned out to be consistent with the reality of the situation. Whenever you experience failure, setbacks, and resistance, it usually means that there is something wrong with your basic premises, your assumptions.

Many people go broke starting their own businesses because they assume that there is a large enough market for the product or service that they propose to offer. They assume that customers will switch from their current suppliers to them for no other reason than they are in the marketplace. They sometimes assume that they have the talents, skills, and abilities to provide the product or service at a competitive price and still make a profit. None of these assumptions may be correct. If even one is false, it can lead to financial ruin.

Your willingness to question your assumptions, to test your assumptions against reality, combined with the willingness to accept the possibility that you could be wrong, is the kind of attitude that will ultimately lead you to great achievement. Flexibility is perhaps the most important single quality you can develop to succeed in business in our fast-changing economy. It is the mark of the superior mind.

How you can apply this law immediately:

1. Identify your most cherished assumptions in the most important areas of your business and personal life. What if they were wrong? What would you do differently from what you are doing today? What are your options?

2. List the five worst things that could happen in your personal or business life in the next year. What would you do if one or more of them occurred? Make a list of options for each emergency and begin thinking about alternate courses of action to the most important things you are dealing with today.

19. The Law of Persistence

—∿∿—

Your ability to persist in the face of setbacks and disappointments is your measure of your belief in yourself and your ability to succeed.

Persistence is the iron quality of success. The most important asset you can have—the one quality that separates you from everyone else—is your ability to persist longer than anyone else.

The first corollary of the Law of Persistence is
Persistence is self-discipline in action.

When you persist in the face of the inevitable setbacks, delays, disappointments, and temporary defeats you will experience in life, and you continue to persist in spite of them, you demonstrate to yourself and to the people around you that you have the qualities of self-discipline and self-mastery that are absolutely indispensable for the achievement of any great success.

Winston Churchill summarized the most important lesson of his life in the second corollary of the Law of Persistence when he said,
"Never give in; never, never, give in."

Churchill believed, and proved again and again throughout his lifetime, that bulldog tenacity in the face of what appeared to be overwhelming defeat was often the critical quality that turned that defeat into victory. Churchill is considered to be perhaps the greatest statesman of the twentieth century because of his willingness to endure without complaint and to hold on tenaciously in the midst of what seemed to be certain defeat and failure.

When you back all of your goals and plans with unshakable determination and persistence, you will eventually find that there is nothing in the world that can stop you. You will become an irresistible force of nature. Your goals of high achievement will become your realities.

How you can apply this law immediately:

1. Make a list of each of the problems or challenges you are facing right now. In what areas are you feeling discouraged and unsure? In what areas do you need to persist even more than you are today? Keep reminding yourself that "Failure is not an option!"

2. Resolve in advance that, no matter what happens, you will never give up. Remember that if you advance confidently in the direction of your dreams, and you resolve in advance that you will never quit, you must ultimately be a great success.

No one can ever stop you but yourself. Go for it!

Summary

Success is not an accident. Success is the definite result of continuous, persistent action in the unrelenting pursuit of your goals in a manner consistent with universal laws.

If only one or two people had practiced these timeless principles and achieved great success as a result, you could dismiss their experiences as luck or coincidence. But if hundreds of thousands, and even millions, of men and women have started with nothing and built wonderful lives by harmonizing their behavior with these laws, wouldn't it be a good idea for you to do the same?

Successful people are not necessarily smarter or better than others. They have just discovered the underlying principles of success and begun applying them before others have. Now you can catch up, and faster than you might have thought possible. When you begin practicing these laws every day, in everything you do, you will begin to make progress faster and easier than ever before.

There are really no limits except the ones you place on yourself by your own thinking.

CHAPTER THREE

The Laws of Business

—✶—

20. The Law of Purpose

21. The Law of Organization

22. The Law of Customer Satisfaction

23. The Law of the Customer

24. The Law of Quality

25. The Law of Obsolescence

26. The Law of Innovation

27. The Law of Critical Success Factors

28. The Law of the Market

29. The Law of Specialization

30. The Law of Differentiation

31. The Law of Segmentation

32. The Law of Concentration

33. The Law of Excellence

The Laws of Business

—∿—

President Calvin Coolidge once said, "The business of America is business." Most of your opportunities for great success in life will come in owning or working for a private business organization. The sooner you learn the laws of business and harmonize your activities with them, the more you will be paid and the faster you will be promoted.

There are more than 23 million businesses in the United States today. Somewhere between 600,000 and 1,000,000 new businesses are being incorporated each year, in addition to hundreds of thousands of sole proprietorships and partnerships that are not registered. These businesses are of every conceivable size and structure, from the single individual working from his or her kitchen table to the largest corporate organization employing hundreds of thousands of people.

Our business system is very much a part of our way of life. Your ability to understand how this amazing system works is essential to your achieving all that is possible for you in our society. This knowledge can help you to be far more successful than people who never take the time to learn.

The rate of change today in business is incredible, and if anything, it is accelerating. Companies are emerging from nowhere, growing rapidly, going public at values of billions of dollars, and then going out of business or being taken over all in a matter of a few short years. We have never seen anything like it before. This incredible rate of change is the one unavoidable and inevitable fact of modern business life.

Each year, as many as 100 companies join or fall off the list of the 500 largest companies in America. Many other corporate giants are either broken up, merged, or acquired or change their major line of business. Everywhere we see huge mergers and mega-mergers that are transforming the world of business and affecting the lives of millions of people.

When we experience this much turbulence amongst the largest and most powerful corporations in the country, you can imagine the kind of turbulence that is being experienced amongst the millions of smaller companies.

Fully 80 percent of new businesses close down or disappear within the first two years of start-up, and many large, established companies go bankrupt or are taken over by other organizations every year.

At the same time, thousands of new companies succeed and many larger companies grow at tremendous rates, despite their sizes. This rate of change means that there are unlimited opportunities for the creative minority, the ones who know the laws of business success. By applying these laws and principles, you increase your ability to make a significant contribution to your organization. You put your life and your career onto the fast track. You make more progress in a couple of years than many people make in their entire careers.

I began learning these principles many years ago. My business career began when I started selling soap for the local YMCA at the age of ten. From there I went on to selling newspapers, lawn-mowing services, and Christmas trees. I worked in a department store as a stock clerk. I later sold office supplies door-to-door and then went on to selling mutual funds, real estate, automobiles, advertising, training, and consulting. I have worked for, sold for, and managed twenty-two organizations of various sizes over the course of more than twenty-five years. I've seen both exciting successes and spectacular failures.

When I was thirty-one, even though I had failed to graduate from high school, I applied for and was accepted into an Executive MBA program at a large university, largely on the basis of my life experiences. For three solid years of evenings, weekends, summers, and two full-time semesters, I put my head down and waded through undergraduate and graduate courses in every facet of business and business management. I came out the other end with a head full of theoretical knowledge and an eagerness to apply some of those ideas to the real world.

Then I had one of the luckiest breaks of my life. I was invited to work as the personal consultant to the chairman of a $500 million conglomerate. By applying some of the laws and principles contained in this chapter, I set up, managed, operated, and generated tens of millions of dollars in sales of various products and services. At every stage of this phase of my business career, the chairman guided me with the advice and insights that had enabled him to become one of the richest and most respected men in the country.

Three years later, I was hired away at triple the salary plus stock options to become the chief operating officer of a $265 million development company. In that position, I applied many of the lessons I'd learned at the knee of the chairman. As a result, I was able to reorganize, redirect, and restaff the company completely within six months.

During this reorganization, I learned a vital principle of business: Any kind of rapid change in a business disrupts the existing power structure, and people will fight viciously to preserve their perks and positions, even to the detriment of the organization. No matter what they say or recommend, people do not like change or change agents. I became the victim of a "palace coup" and soon found myself back on the street, looking for another job.

Over the years, I have seen many kinds of businesses, from the best thought out to the most ridiculous. I have worked with virtually every kind of businessperson, from the most accomplished and skillful to the most foolish and self-deluded. I've read hundreds of books and thousands of articles on various aspects of business and business management, and I still believe that I am only scratching the surface.

Nonetheless, I've developed a few guidelines that have been instrumental in enabling me to build successful businesses of my own. I have also been able to help many of my clients dramatically improve their rates of growth, their market share, and their profitability.

Several laws apply specifically to any business. Your practicing just one of these laws where you may not have in the past can make all the difference to your long-term success. These laws are proven, practical, simple, and effective. Like a treadmill, the more often you use them, the better results you will get.

20. The Law of Purpose

—ᗰ—

The purpose of a business is to create and keep a customer.

Many people think that the purpose of a business is to make a profit. However, while that may be the purpose of the individual who starts or invests in the business, a business is really a separate entity that has a purpose of its own. In fact, a good way to assess the purpose for the existence of a business is to imagine that the owners of the business had to appear in front of a tribunal each year and justify getting permission for the business to carry on. You will see immediately that "making a profit" would not be enough of a reason for the enterprise to justify its continued existence.

The first corollary of the Law of Purpose is

Profits are a measure of how well the company is fulfilling its purpose.

You can tell that customer creation is the primary purpose of a business by simply observing that the majority of the time and attention of the most important people in any successful company is focused on the creation and keeping of customers. The level of sales and profitability that the company enjoys is the result or measure of how well the organization, and everyone in the organization, contributes toward the achievement of that purpose.

The second corollary of the Law of Purpose in business is

Profits are a cost of doing business, the cost of the future.

Many people are confused about the role of profit. Some of them feel that profit, or even the pursuit of profit, is somehow associated with "greed." The fact is that profits are good. It is profits that pay for everything. It is profits that pay for wages and salaries, taxes, investment in new products and processes, research and development, and all the many constructive things that a company can do when it is serving its customers well.

The opposite of profit is loss. Where there are losses, there are reductions in economic activity, fewer jobs, and often the collapse of the enterprise. Where there are continuous losses in a business, there is no future for the people who work there. Anyone who is opposed to profit making is therefore opposed to the future of the people who depend upon that business for their livelihood. These people cannot have a future where there are no profits.

Some people feel that profits are too high. Over an eighty-year period, however, from 1920 to 2000, the largest companies in America have averaged annual after-tax profits of approximately

5 percent per year. Of the total expenditures of most companies, less the costs of raw materials for manufacture or goods for resale, almost 85 percent of all costs are wages, salaries, and bonuses. Wherever a country, or even a part of a country, has lots of profitable companies, it usually has lots of well-paying jobs and great opportunities for the people working at those jobs.

How you can apply this law immediately:

1. Look for opportunities to make your company more successful. Your ability to impact the profitability of your company is the critical determinant of your long-term success. Do you know the price and profit structure of your enterprise? What are your most profitable products? Who are your most profitable customers? Where do you have an influence on the money coming into the company?

2. Identify the areas where you can help create and keep new customers. Look for opportunities to develop and promote new products and services. Find ways to build greater loyalty among your existing customers. Do something every day that increases your company's ability to create and keep customers.

21. The Law of Organization

—⚏—

A business organization is a group of people brought together for the common purpose of creating and keeping customers.

A business organization begins to form when the tasks that must be done to create and satisfy customers become too great for a single person. The founders must specialize and focus on the essential jobs that only they can do and delegate those jobs that can be done by others. New positions are then created, and new activities are undertaken. The company expands its capacity to serve its customers. This growth process continues as long as the increase in people continues to increase the number of customers who are satisfied by that organization.

How you can apply this law immediately:

1. Determine your primary output responsibility, defined in terms of how you contribute to the company's ability to serve customers.

2. Identify how your job is changing within your organization. Determine the changes you will have to make in your knowledge, skills, and activities to remain valuable, if not indispensable, to your company. Make a plan today to increase your ability to contribute to the critical results that determine your company's success.

22. The Law of Customer Satisfaction

—ʍ—

The customer is always right.

This is also called "rule number one" of customer satisfaction. We live in a customer-centered market economy. Never has the customer had so much information and so much power. Every company, large and small, must be thinking day and night about how to please customers faster, better, and cheaper than the competition.

The first corollary of the Law of Customer Satisfaction is

If ever the customer seems to be wrong, refer back to rule number one.

The very best companies in America, and worldwide, are built on this philosophy. They have an obsession with customer service. They are continually looking for ways to please their customers better than any of their competitors and better than even they themselves were pleasing their customers before. In every industry, the most successful companies are those for whom the customer is king or queen and customer satisfaction is the driving force of all their activities.

The second corollary of the Law of Customer Satisfaction is

All customer satisfaction comes from people dealing with other people.

You cannot satisfy people with goods or paper of any kind. People are emotional, and they can be satisfied only as the result of their interactions with other people. According to a Harvard study, fully 68 percent of dissatisfied customers who changed suppliers did so because of the *indifference* of one or more people in the company. This is why the most successful companies have very clear customer satisfaction policies, usually in writing. Everyone in those organizations is committed to treating customers well.

For example, the Walt Disney Corporation hires thousands of college students to work at the Disney theme parks in the summertime. These students are hired in the middle of May and trained for four to six weeks in their functions. They then work for approximately eight weeks of the summer season when children are out of school and the theme parks are the busiest.

When the Disney people are asked why it is that the students receive such rigorous training, lasting four to six weeks, to then work for only eight weeks before going back to school, their reply reveals a lot about the Disney philosophy. Disney executives explain that the students are drilled in their jobs to the point where they can do them without thinking. This allows them to concentrate their attention on the visitors, or "guests," as they are called. Because the students have memorized their jobs completely, they are more conscious of the small things they can do to make people happy that they have chosen to come to a Disney amusement park.

The third corollary of the Law of Customer Satisfaction is

The best companies invariably have the best people.

The best companies learned a long time ago that the people they select will largely determine their success. They therefore take a long time to hire people and are very careful in both interviewing and in checking references. Once a person has been hired, if that hiree is the wrong person, he or she can cause a great deal of harm before being let go.

Your ability to attract and keep good people is vital to your long-term success as an executive. Fortunately, you can learn how to interview and hire well. This is a key skill for success in business.

The fourth corollary of the Law of Customer Satisfaction is

The key role of management is to achieve the maximum return on investment in human resources toward satisfying customers.

You have two choices with any job. You can either do the job yourself or you can get someone else to do it. As a manager, your job is to get things done through others rather than doing them yourself.

One final observation on customer satisfaction: The employees of a company will always treat the customers the way the management treats the employees. Whenever you are treated especially well by people in any store or restaurant, you know that that place has a good manager who treats the staff well. Whenever you are treated poorly, for any reason, you know that the person you are dealing with is probably treating you this way in an attempt to get back at a manager who she feels is treating her badly.

How you can apply this law immediately:

1. Resolve today to give your customers the very highest quality and quantity of service in the industry. Never be satisfied with second best.

2. Determine where you and your company rank based on the four levels of customer satisfaction described below. Develop a plan of action to move toward the highest levels.

Here are the four levels of customer satisfaction. The first, the bare minimum for survival, is *meeting* customer expectations. What are the basic expectations of your customers, and how could you meet them with greater consistency?

The second level of customer satisfaction is where you *exceed* customer expectations. What additional service features could you create that would go beyond what your competitors are doing?

The third level is where you *delight* your customers. What could you do that would pleasantly surprise your customers, something completely beyond their expectations?

Finally, the fourth level of customer satisfaction, reached only by the most successful and respected organizations, is where you *amaze* your customers. This is where you are so good at going beyond anything they would expect that not only do they buy from you again and again, but they tell their friends to buy from you as well. In what ways could you design your customer relation policies so that you amaze your customers?

23. The Law of the Customer

—∞—

The customer always acts to satisfy his or her interests by seeking the very most and best at the lowest possible price.

Customers practice economic calculation in their choices. They seek to maximize their purchases and to minimize their costs, or outlays. Customers always attempt to get the things they want the fastest and easiest way possible, right now, at the lowest possible price.

This is not a problem. This is merely a fact of business life. Customers want the very most for the very least, and they will buy from whoever they feel can best give it to them. And they are always right. To survive and thrive in business, you must deal daily with completely self-centered, capricious, impatient customers who want what they want, when and how they want it, and who will go elsewhere at a moment's notice. Just like you.

By the way, it is important to distinguish between *facts* and *problems*. They are quite different, and confusion over which is which can cause you a lot of stress.

A fact, by definition, just is. It is an inevitable and unavoidable part of life. It is something that you accept and work with and around, like the weather. It is like an immovable object. You don't argue with it or get upset about a fact.

A problem, on the other hand, is something that you can solve. A problem is something that is amenable to your intelligence and imagination.

It is very important, in business, that you separate facts from problems and that you don't become upset or anxious over something about which you can do nothing. One of Burnham's Laws, from the philosopher James Burnham, deals with this difference between facts and problems. It says, "If there is no alternative, there is no problem."

Before you become concerned about something that has or has not happened, ask yourself, Is this a problem, or is this a fact? Past events, by the way, are all facts. The only effect you can have on them is the way you interpret them and react to them. What matters is what you do *now*, not what happened or who is to blame or what you could have done differently.

The first corollary of the Law of the Customer is

Customers are both demanding and ruthless; they
reward highly those companies that serve them
best and allow those companies that serve them
poorly to fail.

Sam Walton once said, "We all have the same boss, the customer, and he can fire us any time he wants by deciding to buy somewhere else."

It isn't that customers don't care about your business. It's just that customers care more about themselves and their own satisfaction than they do about the success or failure of your enterprise. Wherever you see a business fail, you see a business where the owners were either unable or unwilling to adjust their offerings to satisfy enough customers at prices that allowed them to carry on. The customers silently walked away, told their friends about their bad experiences, and never came back.

The second corollary of this law is
Customers always behave rationally in pursuing the
path of least resistance to get what they want.

From the point of view of the customer, every action makes
perfect sense. All buying behavior is aimed at achieving greater
personal satisfaction, toward improving one's position, toward
being better off. If a salesperson or a businessperson suggests that
the customers are stupid for not patronizing a particular store or
buying its products, it is actually the salesperson or the businessperson who is stupid.

The customer is very smart and usually knows what is in his
or her best interests. The customer's decision is always rational,
from the customer's point of view. The customer is always right,
as far as the customer is concerned. When you go into business,
you put your entire financial future at the mercy of satisfying your
customers every single day. From the moment you open your
doors, the customer determines what you will sell, how much of
it you will sell, at what price you will sell it, and how much money
you will make. It is only by catering to the customer's whims and
desires that you can survive and thrive in business.

The third corollary of the Law of the Customer is
Proper business planning always begins with the
customer as the central focus of attention and
discussion.

People within companies have a dangerous tendency to lose
touch with the thoughts, feelings, and needs of their customers.
They tend to talk only among themselves, and what is worse, they
listen only to each other. They lose touch with the reality of their
customers.

If you are in business, and if what you do affects your customer, you should mentally erect a statue of the customer and

place it in the middle of the table when you discuss any plans regarding your products or services. Always ask yourself, If the customer was sitting here listening to us, what would the customer be thinking? What would the customer say? Would the customer approve or disapprove of what we're planning to do?

By the way, the subject of the "customer" is very important. Some people within organizations have the mistaken idea that they have no customers because they don't interact with the people who buy the product or service from the company. This can be a fatal mistake in thinking. It can sabotage your career without your even knowing it.

The fact is that everyone has a customer, and many people have several. Your primary customer is the person who determines how much you are paid and how quickly you are promoted. By this definition, unless you are the owner yourself, your primary customer is your boss. How well you please your boss determines how far and how fast you move ahead.

If you are a manager and you have people working under you, your staff members are also your customers. How you treat them and satisfy them will determine how they satisfy your customers.

If you work in accounting or administration, your customers are the people who must use what you produce, whether it be financial statements, computer printouts, or other information.

Everyone has a customer. Everyone is in the business of customer satisfaction. Your level of success in business is determined by how well you satisfy your most important customers.

How you can apply this law immediately:

1. Make a list of all your customers, both inside and outside of your business. Write down the names of your boss and coworkers, your outside customers and contacts, everyone with whom you deal, including your staff.

2. Make a plan today to increase your value to the most important of these people in some way. What results would you ideally like to achieve in your relationships with these customers?

Resolve to do something every day to increase the level of satisfaction your key customers enjoy when dealing with you and your company.

24. The Law of Quality
—∞—

The customer demands the very highest quality for the very lowest price.

This seems simple except that many companies try to violate this law on their way to the bankruptcy courts. The customer is very smart. The customer will always act to satisfy the greatest possible number of his or her needs in making any particular buying decision. Only companies that cater to the customer's relentless insistence on ever-higher levels of quality at ever-lower prices are successful in the marketplace.

In 1989, both the Toyota Lexus and the Nissan Infiniti were introduced into the U.S. market. Both companies advertised these cars as the cars of the future, with the luxury features of the more expensive European cars but at prices that were $10,000, $20,000, or $30,000 cheaper. Both companies committed themselves to offering the finest quality automobiles in their class in America.

And they succeeded. From 1991 onward, the J. D. Power Survey of Customer Satisfaction has consistently rated Lexus and Infiniti among the best cars, in terms of vehicle quality and after-sales service, among all 557 models of automobiles sold in the United States. Repeatedly, J. D. Power rankings have the Lexus and the Infiniti tied for first place in quality amongst all cars sold in the country.

As a result of these quality rankings, the sales of these cars consistently amount to hundreds of millions of dollars each year.

The first corollary of the Law of Quality is

Quality is what the customer says it is and is willing
to pay for.

Only the customer can define quality. Sometimes even the customer cannot define it clearly, but the customer will vote for quality by the way she spends her dollars. And more than 80 percent of buying decisions today are either made or strongly influenced by women.

Philip Crosby, in his book *Quality without Tears*, wrote, "Quality is fairly easy to define. The quality of a product can be measured by what percentage of the time it does what it is sold to do and continues to do it."

You can measure the quality of a watch by how long it continues to tell perfect time. If it does so 100 percent of the time without stopping, it would have a 100 percent quality rating.

If you buy a car, the quality rating of that car is how long it continues to give you trouble-free service, without needing repairs, aside from those specified at the time of purchase. If the car runs trouble-free for 100 percent of the time, it has a 100 percent quality rating.

Unfortunately, it is not uncommon for fully 25 percent of products manufactured today to have to be reworked and rebuilt right at the factory because of quality defects. Philip Crosby's book title *Quality Is Free* is based on his conclusion that manufacturing a high-quality item, without defects, actually saves money and boosts profits, both in the short term and in the long term. In the short term, quality creates customers, and in the long term, a reputation for quality keeps customers.

The second corollary of the Law of Quality is
Quality includes both the product or service and
the way that it is sold, delivered, and maintained.

The customer's definition of quality includes all of the activities associated with the purchase, ownership, and use of the item.

Prices in a quality restaurant are not based only on the fact that good food is served on a plate. A first-class restaurant, one that commands above-average prices and can earn above-average profits, also serves the food in an atmosphere of comfort and enjoyment that people are willing to pay more for. Can you imagine a waiter in a nice restaurant slapping the plate down on the table and just walking away?

Even a simple product can be sold and served with cheerfulness and courtesy, thereby increasing its perceived value. The total experience the customer enjoys is all part of the impression of quality.

The third corollary of the Law of Quality is
Companies are profitable in direct proportion to
their quality ranking, as customers perceive it.

What this means is that if a research firm was to go into your marketplace and conduct an honest, objective survey amongst the customers for what you sell, it could develop a quality ranking for your company in terms of how it compares to your competitors.

For example, suppose ten companies are offering the same product in the same market area. A survey of customers would reveal which of these companies is perceived to be the very best company in that industry in that market. The survey would also be able to determine which company would rank as number two, number three, and so on. The companies that were perceived to be the highest-quality companies in that market would also turn out to be the most profitable companies in that market.

A major reason that companies that are seen as high-quality companies are more profitable is because of the deep need that customers have for security or safety in their purchase decisions. Whenever people have to make a choice between a higher priced product and a lower priced product, if they can possibly afford it, they will choose the higher priced product because a higher price is associated with better quality. Better quality is associated in the customers' minds with greater safety and predictability. The perception of better quality reduces the feeling of uncertainty or risk in making the buying decision. It makes it easier to buy.

That's why it is said, "If you can afford to buy quality, you can't afford not to." There is almost always a direct relationship between the amount that you pay and the quality of the product or service that you receive. You very seldom get good quality at a low price. You never get something for nothing. You always get what you pay for. In a competitive society you can safely assume that paying a higher price will assure you a higher level of quality and a lower level of risk.

Remember what Thomas Ruskin said: "The bitterness of poor quality is remembered long after the pleasure of low price has been forgotten."

Wherever your business stands in the quality rankings, and almost everyone knows intuitively where his or her business ranks, even without a survey, you must commit yourself and your company to the number one position. You must commit to becoming the very best in your chosen field.

Aim for quality leadership in your product or service. The commitment to quality will not only animate and excite everyone in the organization, but it will also be reflected in the profits that flow to your bottom line. The companies with the highest quality are the companies that earn the highest profits. They represent the greatest opportunities for the future.

How you can apply this law immediately:

1. Determine your quality ranking in your industry. Use objective polling if you can. Use your intuition if you must. But be absolutely honest with yourself. Ask your staff and colleagues where they would rank your company on a scale from one to ten among your competitors, as well.

2. Determine exactly how your customers define quality. Find out what level of quality they expect from you. Critically examine your products and services and how you sell and support them. Ask your best customers what they most value about your business and how you could improve in that area.

3. Select one critical area to focus on for improvement. Pick an area or activity that has a direct bearing on customer satisfaction. Resolve to be the best in this one area. Tell everyone in your company about this commitment and then measure yourself regularly to see how well you are progressing.

25. The Law of Obsolescence

—␣m␣—

Whatever exists is already becoming obsolete.

The Law of Obsolescence says that everything—products, services, skills, core competencies, advertisements, marketing strategies, and business processes—is becoming obsolete with the passing of time. To survive and thrive in these times of turbulence, you and your company must be fast on your feet and prepared to deal with continual change as an unavoidable fact of life.

The first corollary of the Law of Obsolescence is
Tomorrow will be different from today.

The most frustrated people in business today are those who are trying to hold back the tide of change by failing to adapt, or by adapting too slowly to the competitive onslaught that is taking place all around them.

The second corollary of this law is
Continuing innovation and improvement are essential to survival.

Innovation and improvement are not things you do when you have enough time and money. Every company must have its top people dedicated to developing the products and services of tomorrow. If a company does not commit itself to continuous innovation, it will find itself with a shaky present and an uncertain future. It will simply be left in the dust by competitors who are eager to take its business.

The most successful companies, under virtually all economic conditions, are those that continually innovate and introduce new products and services, even when business is slow. There seems to be a direct relationship between the quantity of new ideas the company attempts and the ultimate financial success of the business.

The third corollary of the Law of Obsolescence is
The best way to predict the future is to create it.

When Walt Disney was asked if he was worried about people copying his ideas, he replied by saying, "Don't worry! We'll come up with new ideas faster than anyone can possibly steal them."

This should be your philosophy, as well. You should always have more ideas for new products and services than you possibly have time or resources to develop. You should then examine the entire range of possibilities to choose the ones that have the greatest market potential at that moment.

Be open to everyone's ideas. A person working in a company can often see a need for a product or service that can revolutionize both the company and the industry. You probably know the story of the scientist at 3M Corporation in Minnesota who was having a tough time getting a bookmark to stick in the pages of his hymnbook. He experimented with a variety of glues, looking for an adhesive that would enable a piece of paper to stick on and come off several times without leaving a mark or losing its stickiness.

He finally developed the adhesive that led to today's Post-it notes. 3M Corporation now dominates the world market for stick-on notes and sells several hundred million dollars' worth of this product each year. And because of profit sharing, the researcher who came up with the idea has become a wealthy man.

How you can apply this law immediately:

1. Imagine that your highest-volume, highest-profit product will be obsolete within three to five years. What new products or services could you develop and market to take its place?

2. Imagine that your business burned to the ground overnight and you were tasked with getting new facilities and starting over. What would you do differently?

26. The Law of Innovation

—ᴍ—

All breakthroughs in business come from
innovation, from offering something better,
cheaper, faster, newer, or more efficient in
the current marketplace.

In Peter Drucker's book *Innovation and Entrepreneurship*, he
discusses the seven major sources of innovation in business. He
explains several ideas you can use to make innovation a way of life,
both for yourself and for your business.

The two major sources of innovation, according to Drucker,
are *unexpected success* and *unexpected failure*. In the case of either,
you must carefully analyze what happened to determine if a potential breakthrough has occurred.

The "tip of the iceberg" theory of critical thinking is especially
helpful in examining successes, failures, or any unexpected events.
Whenever something out of the ordinary happens, stop and ask,
Is this a single event, or is it the tip of an iceberg? Could this be
the beginning of a trend, indicating a major shift in the marketplace? Many great business breakthroughs occur as the result of
recognizing a trend in the market and then moving before anyone
else to take advantage of it or, conversely, recognizing a trend away
from your product or service and moving to minimize your expo-
sure and develop other products or services while you still have
time.

Perhaps the most significant trend of our age is the movement
toward personal computers and the Internet. When the first personal computer was developed, IBM did its own research on the
future of this product. IBM consultants came to the conclusion
that the total world market for personal computers was only 300
or 400 units per year. The company decided to stick to main-

frames. Today, more than 50 million personal computers are sold each year, and mainframes have become secondary to the computer revolution. IBM ignored the tip of the iceberg!

How you can apply this law immediately:

1. Identify and analyze the trends in your business. Where are sales growing or declining? What are your customers telling you they want more of? Less of? What should you be getting into or out of?

2. Admire your successful competitors! Where and how are your most successful competitors achieving the greatest sales and profitability? What are they doing that you could learn from and improve upon?

3. Analyze your biggest successes and failures of the previous year. What valuable lessons do they contain that you can use to your best advantage in the months and years ahead? Remember that all great success is preceded by failure, and every failure contains valuable lessons you can learn from. What are yours?

27. The Law of Critical Success Factors

—∞—

Every business has a number of key success factors that measure and determine its success or failure.

Critical success factors in business are like the vital functions of the body, such as heart rate, respiratory rate, blood pressure, brain-wave activity, and so on. These vital functions are all indicators and measures of the overall health and vitality of an individual. The absence of any one of them, even for a few moments, can lead to the death of an individual.

Companies have critical success factors, as well, which measure the health and vitality of an enterprise. Many of these are common to all businesses. In addition, some companies will have critical success factors that are unique to that organization.

The most common critical success factors in business are leadership, product quality, service, sales, marketing, manufacturing, distribution, and finance and accounting. Excellent performance is necessary in every one of these areas for a company to enjoy excellent results. Poor performance, or nonperformance, in any one of these areas can threaten the survival of a business.

For example, according to Dun and Bradstreet, the majority of business failures in the United States are triggered by a drop-off in sales and sales revenue. Whatever the causes of low sales, any prolonged weakness in this area can lead to the collapse of the enterprise. This, then, is a critical success factor, or a vital function of a business.

The first corollary of this law is
Each individual has personal critical success factors,
the performance of which determines his or her
business future.

You have a set of key skills or core competencies that you use, like tools, to do your job. A weakness or failure in any one of your key skills can undermine your overall effectiveness and weaken your ability to do your job effectively. To perform at your best, you must first identify the critical success factors of your work, measure your strengths in each one, and then develop a plan to become excellent in the areas that can help you the most.

For example, problem solving and decision making are critical success factors for every person in business. These are core competencies that are central to all business activities. If a person is physically ill or experiencing a difficult emotional situation in his or her life, that person may not be capable of solving problems intelligently or making good decisions. Everyone who then depends upon that person to think and decide effectively is at risk. An entire department can be negatively impacted because of a weakness in one critical success factor in a key person.

Within each key performance area, there are also critical success factors. For example, in selling, a weakness in a single one of the critical success factors can reduce a salesperson's effectiveness, causing that person to sell only a small part of what he or she is capable of selling. In many companies, the sales force has been poorly trained or not trained at all. The members of senior management cannot figure out why they are not getting the kind of sales that they want or expect. Sometimes, by focusing in on a particular critical success factor, sales training can double or even triple the sales of a business.

To determine your personal critical success factors, ask yourself two questions. The first question is, Why am I on the payroll?

What, exactly, have you been hired to accomplish? Why does the company pay you the money it does? Both you and your boss should be in complete agreement on this question. Whatever your answer is to this question, that is what you should be working on most of the time.

The second question is, What can I, and only I, do that if done well will make a real difference to my company?

This is a task or responsibility that only you can do. If you don't do it, it won't get done. But if you do do it, and do it well, it can make a tremendous difference both to your company and to yourself.

These are questions that you should ask each day: Why am I on the payroll? and What can I, and only I, do that if done well will make a real difference? They should be asked of every single person in an organization on a regular basis. Everyone should be absolutely clear about the answers. This is one way to assure that each person is focusing his or her very best efforts in the areas of personal critical success factors.

The second corollary of this law is
Your weakest critical success factor determines the height at which you can use all your other skills.

Your personal strengths and core competencies are what have brought you to where you are today. They are the foundations of your position and the determinants of your income. At the same time, your weaknesses form the ceiling on your ability to rise to even greater heights. Your weakest critical success factor sets the limit on how far and how fast you can go. It acts likes a brake on your potential.

To move ahead more rapidly, you must be brutally honest with yourself in seeking out and facing your areas of weakness. What are they? *What one skill, if you developed and did it in an excellent fashion, would have the greatest positive impact on your career?* Whatever the answer to this question, this is where you should begin to work on yourself. This is where you can get the biggest payoff in terms of increased competence.

How you can apply this law immediately:

1. Look upon yourself as a work in progress. You have come a long way, but you still have a long way to go. What are the critical success factors of your company, the areas of activity where you absolutely, positively have to be excellent to be the best in your particular business?

2. Identify the critical success factors of the key people in your organization. What are the strengths that are responsible for

their successes to date? Their weaknesses, especially personal weaknesses, usually lie at the root of most of your problems.

3. What are your personal critical success factors, and what is your plan to become absolutely excellent in the one area that can help you the most at this time? Whatever it is, begin immediately to work on yourself in that area, and don't stop until you've mastered this key skill.

28. The Law of the Market

—m—

The market is where buyers and sellers of products and services meet to set prices and determine the allocation of money, labor, materials, and all factors of production.

The market is a fictitious place, existing everywhere and nowhere. The market represents all of the millions of buying and selling decisions that take place every day at every level of society and in every area of private and public enterprise. The sum total of all of these decisions determines the prices of virtually everything that is not government controlled in our society.

The first corollary of the Law of the Market is
In a free market, resources will be allocated with complete efficiency and prices will accurately reflect supply and demand to that moment.

This "efficient-market thesis," usually applied to the stock market, says that all stock prices at the close of each day will accurately reflect all the information that is known about the present and future prospects of the companies represented by the shares. This thesis also says that knowledge of factors affecting prices will spread rapidly to those people whose economic interests are involved.

The second corollary of the Law of the Market is

The free market is the most efficient way for millions of people to have their needs met at the lowest possible cost.

The free market is perhaps the greatest miracle of all of human experience and human society. The free market forms spontaneously and operates automatically virtually everywhere—in the absence of government interference in economic activities or economic decision making. The freer the market, the more vibrant the economy and the greater the quantity of wealth and opportunity that is created for more people.

In Hong Kong, for example, there are virtually no government regulations, aside from traffic and police protection. The highest tax rate on income, personal or corporate, is 20 percent. Hong Kong is a tiny area with no natural resources. The former British colony contains approximately 5 million people living in a small space. Nevertheless, in the absence of government interference, it enjoys one of the most buoyant economies in the world. The little peninsula and island has produced countless millionaires and several billionaires. As the result of free markets, Hong Kong is so prosperous that it regularly suffers from labor shortages.

The third corollary of the Law of the Market is

The freer the market is from government interference, the greater the supply and variety of goods and services and the greater the prosperity of the people.

Each year, the Heritage Foundation of Washington, D.C., publishes its Index of Economic Freedom, ranking all the countries of the world on a scale from "most free" to "least free." Year after year, in comparison after comparison, this and other studies show that the health, wealth, general prosperity, and economic opportunity of the average person is higher in direct proportion to the openness of markets and the freedom of business from government interference and regulation.

Every intervention of the government in the freedom of the marketplace is made for a reason that sounds good and is ostensibly for the good of the public. But the real reason is usually to benefit or bribe some special interest or favored constituency. Each government interference ends up raising prices or reducing supply, ultimately penalizing customers by forcing them to pay more for a product or service than they would have had to if the market were unrestricted. To put it another way, interference in the marketplace seldom ever reduces prices for anyone on any product or service over the long term. Its purpose is usually exactly the opposite.

Business success depends upon your ability to enter the market with products and services that you can sell in competition with other similar products and services offered by your competitors. The free market enables a person to start with nothing but an idea, backed by energy and ambition, and build a great enterprise. One of your duties is to protect and defend this system by understanding it and supporting it when it comes under attack.

How you can apply this law immediately:

1. Become a champion of the free market. Recognize that open markets—where the customer is king or queen and all business success is dependent on serving customers with the things they want, at the highest possible quality and at the lowest possible price—are the best hope for opportunity and prosperity for the greatest number of people.

2. Study the other markets of the world and keep alert for new products and services, or innovative ways of offering or

improving existing products and services, that you could copy
and apply to your business. One good idea is all you need to
give yourself the winning edge in your industry.

29. The Law of Specialization

—⚭—

To succeed in a competitive marketplace, a
product or service must be specialized to
perform a specific function and be excellent
at satisfying a clearly defined need of the
customer.

It must be clear what the product is uniquely suited to do and
for whom the product is designed. Products that try to be all
things to all customers end up being nothing to no one. If customers are unsure of the specific use or application of the product,
they will pass it by in favor of something else.

The first corollary of the Law of Specialization is
Companies fail when they no longer specialize and
do not serve a sufficient number of customers in a
cost-effective way.

Specialization is the starting point of successful marketing. It
must be made clear what it is you are offering and to whom.
Carefully and continually defining and redefining your specific
customer is absolutely essential for the success of your business. A
slight change or shift in your customer base or customer focus can
have a dramatic effect on your sales, upward or downward.

Hundreds of models of automobiles are offered for sale every
year. Each of these models is designed for a special type of person,
with certain tastes, experiences, income, education, and needs.

Companies such as Toyota, Ford, and DaimlerChrysler succeed greatly because they design each model to satisfy the special needs and demands of large segments of the automobile market. Other companies struggle and lose money because they fail to specialize their offerings to a large enough customer market.

We see this same ability or failure to specialize in Internet start-ups, where companies with a great idea go public at extraordinary valuations. Within a few months, these companies can turn out to be stars, or shooting stars, to the exact degree to which they have been able to specialize enough to attract a large enough customer base.

How you can apply this law immediately:

1. Continually ask and answer accurately the following questions: Who is our customer? Who exactly is our product designed for? What does our customer consider value? What specific need, want, or desire does our customer have that our product is created to satisfy?

2. Study your market carefully and ask yourself: In what ways could our product or service be modified or improved so that it satisfies even more of the special needs of a larger number of customers? What could we do to our product or service to make it even more appealing to a larger market without losing our core customer base?

30. The Law of Differentiation

—m—

A product or service must have a
competitive advantage or an area of
excellence that enables it to stand out from
its competitors in some way if it is to
succeed in a competitive marketplace.

Your product or service must be unique, better, or even out-standing in some way if you are going to sell it in sufficient quantities to be successful. It cannot be a "me too" product. It has to have special strengths or qualities that make it different from any of the other products or services that compete with it or that can be used as a substitute for it.

The first corollary of the Law of Differentiation is

The determination of a unique selling proposition
(USP) is the starting point of all successful
advertising and sales.

A company should be able to summarize what makes its product or service unique and better in twenty-five words or less. Ford says, "Quality Is Job One." BMW calls its cars "The Ultimate Driving Machine." IBM bases its advertising and marketing on "Quality and Customer Service." Nordstrom is famous, and highly profitable, because of its reputation for "Service." Coca-Cola is "The Real Thing." These advantages convey clearly why someone should choose these companies over a competitor.

The very best marketing, advertising, and selling campaigns are built around a unique selling proposition that can be communicated in a meaningful way to the prospective customer. What is yours?

The second corollary of the Law of Differentiation is
To succeed in the marketplace, a product or service
must have a distinct advantage, something that makes
it superior to competing products and services.

The determination of your competitive advantage for your product or service is perhaps the most important single marketing and selling decision your company makes. Weakness in this area is the biggest single reason for market failure for any product or service.

Whether the product is a national newspaper, like *USA Today,* which lost several hundred million dollars before it eventually pulled into the black, or a candidate for political office, the advertisers must create a meaningful competitive advantage that gives the prospective customer a good reason to buy that product rather than buying something else.

Jack Welch, CEO of General Electric, has said that his philosophy is to be either number one or number two in every product area in which General Electric competes. If General Electric cannot achieve the first or second position within a reasonable time period, it will withdraw from the market and focus its resources in another area where it can dominate. He says, "If you don't have competitive advantage, don't compete."

The success of Internet companies such as Amazon, America Online, Yahoo, eBay, Priceline, and others is due to large numbers of customers perceiving these sites to be superior in design and features to other sites that offer similar services and products.

Your area of excellence, or competitive advantage, can change over time in response to changing market conditions. When market tastes or demands change, you must change as well.

For example, for many years, local restaurants competed on the basis of good food, reasonable prices, and convenient locations. Most still do today. Then, along came young Tom Monahagn in East Lansing, Michigan, with an idea to premake a selection of the most popular pizzas so they could be baked and delivered within a certain geographical area within thirty minutes. Domino's Pizza was born.

There are now several thousand Domino's Pizza restaurants worldwide and Tom Monahagn is a billionaire. He selected an area of competitive advantage, that of *speed* in the delivery of a popular and inexpensive food, and redefined his industry.

How you can apply this law immediately:

1. Define your competitive advantage in one sentence. In what way is your product or service superior to that of your competitors? What makes you special? Write your answer in such simple terms that an intelligent child can understand it and repeat it back to you.

2. Decide today to develop and promote a competitive advantage of some kind, if you don't currently have one. What could it be? What should it be? With the way your market is changing, what will it have to be in the future? Ask your customers what they like best about what you sell them or do for them. This is usually what they perceive to be your competitive difference. Why do they buy from you rather than from your competitors?

31. The Law of Segmentation

—◠◠◠—

Companies must target specific customer groups or market segments if they are to achieve significant sales.

We are rapidly reaching the end of the mass market. Today, the most successful companies are those that have been able to identify specific segments of the marketplace for which they design individualized products and services to satisfy special needs and tastes.

The first corollary of the Law of Segmentation is
Many companies fail because they are targeting the
wrong market with the wrong product in the
wrong way.

Many companies start off targeting their advertising and sales at a particular market segment, only to find that the products are being purchased by a different market segment altogether. Light pickups were originally designed for people doing construction work and hauling around small quantities of materials. They became extremely popular with young people as sports vehicles for going to the beach and mountains.

For many years, the German beer Lowenbrau, a high-priced import, tried to compete with American beers such as Budweiser and Miller. The company tried every conceivable form of advertising and was still unable to break into the American market, which was tied up by the big breweries. Finally, Lowenbrau changed its marketing strategy and began targeting men and women with higher incomes. The first new advertisement changed the whole market for imported beer in the United States. It said, "When you run out of champagne, order Lowenbrau."

By positioning itself against champagne rather than lower-priced beer, Lowenbrau created a perception that imported beer was something to be enjoyed by people who could afford the very best.

The second corollary of the Law of Segmentation is
The ideal market segment contains those customers for whom the product's competitive
advantage is most important in satisfying their
most pressing needs.

In other words, if you are selling food, sell to hungry people. If you are selling time management systems, sell to those whose time is the most valuable and who feel their time is most in need of management.

Your best market segment consists of those who already have a clearly defined and demonstrated need for your product. As they say, "Fish where the fish are."

The whole purpose of market research is for you to identify and segment your market so you can reach it with the greatest efficiency and at the lowest possible cost. The more accurate you are about the customer you are trying to create and keep, the more focused your marketing efforts will be and the more likely it is that they will be successful.

How you can apply this law immediately:

1. Develop a clear profile of your ideal customers. Who are they—exactly? What is their age, sex, education, income, and value base? Where are they? Where do they live geographically? In what sort of businesses and industries do they work? In what positions do they work? In what departments of what types of companies are they located?

2. Determine the very best way to sell to your ideal customer. How do they buy? When do they buy? What sort of selling methods are available to you to communicate with the prospective customers who can benefit the most rapidly from what you sell?

32. The Law of Concentration

—∞—

Market success comes from concentrating single-mindedly on selling to those customers you have segmented as being the ones who can most benefit immediately from the

unique product or service features you offer
in your area of specialization.

To return to the examples of Lexus and Infiniti, these two cars compete in a specific market niche or segment, and their marketing efforts are concentrated on selling to those men and women who can and will pay for a luxury car in the $35,000–$55,000 price range. These are generally well-paid, upwardly mobile, college-educated, white-collar professionals. These are men and women who admire the BMW and the Mercedes-Benz but for whom these cars are out of their price range.

Lexus and Infiniti know that the farther down the price curve they can go with their offerings, the greater the number of potential customers there are within this market segment who will buy the product. While BMW and Mercedes fight it out for the customers who can pay $50,000 to $75,000, Lexus and Infiniti have decided to price their products below those of Jaguar and position themselves in the same area as the highest priced American cars. And their strategy is working for them remarkably well.

The first corollary of the Law of Concentration is
The best high-profit strategy is to dominate a specific market niche with the best product available
for those customers in that niche.

An example of dominating a specific market niche is the strategy pursued by the Cross Pen Company. The company has managed to position the Cross pen in the minds of American businesspeople as the premier, high-quality American business pen. The company has pens that range from inexpensive black models through medium-cost silver and all the way up to 18-karat, all-gold luxury writing instruments. No matter how much Parker or Mont Blanc pens attempt to make inroads in the business market, the Cross pen is considered worldwide to be the quality pen for that particular market niche. This dominance has made the Cross Pen Company one of the most successful and profitable small companies in the world.

The second corollary of the Law of Concentration is

Concentration on high-profit market segments, with high-profit products and services gives the highest return on sales, return on investment, and return on equity.

The most profitable companies are those selling high-profit products in high-profit markets. They focus on dominating their markets and continually seek ways to innovate and improve their offerings.

American car companies make their largest unit profits on cars such as the Chrysler Imperial, the Ford Lincoln Continental, and the Cadillac by General Motors. The companies that manufacture the very best, highest quality, most expensive products invariably earn the highest possible profits on the sales of those products. Rolex Watch Company is another example of this.

How you can apply this law immediately:

1. Examine your entire range of product or service offerings. Which of these are the most expensive and which are the most profitable? Are these the same? How could you sell more of your highest profit products or services?

2. Analyze each of your products and services to determine exactly how much it costs you to produce, sell, and service. Then determine exactly how much net profit you realize from the sale of each item. Which products or services represent a lot of economic activity but yield low net profits?

33. The Law of Excellence

—⟶⟨⟩⟵—

The market pays excellent returns and
rewards for excellent performance, excellent
products, and excellent services.

Customers want the very most for the very least. They prefer higher quality over lower quality because higher quality promises greater satisfaction and fewer problems after purchasing. Companies with high quality ratings can charge more and earn more per sale. A commitment to product or service excellence is the safest and most predictable strategy for achieving business success.

The first corollary of the Law of Excellence is
The market pays average rewards for average
performance and below-average rewards for
below-average performance.

The market is a just taskmaster. It is always fair. It is always equitable. The market always reflects the real valuations of the customer as they are expressed in buying behavior. It always rewards those who serve it with the goods and services it wants at prices it is willing to pay, and it always punishes those companies who refuse to do so by simply declining to buy their offerings.

The key to your earning excellent rewards in your work is for you to become excellent at doing the most important parts of your job as they are defined by your boss and your customers. The key to success in your business is for you to develop a reputation for excellence in everything you do.

How you can apply this law immediately:

1. Commit to excellence in your work, especially in your key result areas and your core competencies. Resolve today to join

the top 10 percent in your field, whatever it is you do. This commitment to top performance will do more to move you into the fast lane in your career than any other decision you can make.

2. Develop a reputation for being the kind of person who is always looking for ways to do things better and faster. Volunteer for assignments and then do them fast. Speed is a key component of excellence, particularly as it is perceived by customers. And the customer is always right.

Summary: The Five Rules for Business Success

The keys to business success have always been the same. A thousand books have been written and countless articles have been published, but they all eventually come back to what I call the "big five."

First, the product or service must be ideally suited to the existing market and to what people want, need, and are willing to pay for. Products or services that are not ideally suited to the demands of the existing market must be changed quickly or run the risk of disappearing.

Second, there must be a companywide focus on marketing, sales, and revenue generation. The most important energies of the most talented people in the company must be centered on the customer and on selling more of your most profitable products to ever-larger numbers of customers. The failure to focus single-mindedly on sales is the number one cause of business failure in any economy.

Third, efficient internal systems of bookkeeping, accounting, inventory management, and cost control must exist. Poor control of operating costs and internal administration is the number two reason for business failure.

Fourth, there must be a clear sense of direction and a high level of synergy and teamwork among the managers and staff in the organization. The company should function like a well-oiled machine, with a place for everyone and everyone in his or her place, performing at his or her best.

Finally, the company should never stop learning, growing, innovating, and improving. The Japanese call this the process of *Kaizen*. W. Edwards Deming, the father of quality in both Japan and America, taught that continuous training and upgrading of skills at all levels of the company is the key to achieving a meaningful competitive advantage and long-term business success.

The American free-enterprise system, where you and I and anyone else have the freedom to enter the marketplace, to attempt to serve customers with goods and services in better ways or at cheaper prices than anyone else, is the finest system ever evolved for the satisfaction of needs and the creation of opportunity.

You can take your place in this system at any time by offering a product or service that people want and are willing to pay for. By practicing these laws of business, you can build a successful company or career that brings you all the rewards and satisfactions you desire in life.

CHAPTER FOUR

The Laws of Leadership
—ₘ—

The Laws of Leadership

—∿—

Leadership is the most important single factor in determining business success or failure in our competitive, turbulent, fast-moving economy. The quality of leadership is the decisive strength or weakness of organizations and institutions. The ability to step up to the plate and provide the necessary leadership is the key determinant of achievement in all human activities. And there has never been a greater need for leaders at all levels than there is today.

The qualities of leadership and the personal attributes of leaders have been studied for more than 2,500 years, going back to Thucydides and his *History of the Peloponnesian War*. There are currently more than 5,000 different books, articles, and commentaries on leaders and leadership, each of which gives insights and ideas into ways that individuals can learn to become better leaders in their personal and business lives.

Perhaps the best news is that leaders are made, not born. A person becomes a leader when a leader is needed and the individual rises to the occasion. Many men and women have lived average lives for many years until a situation arises that requires that they step forward and accept the mantle of leadership, with all that that entails.

You become a leader in your business and in the world around you by practicing the qualities and behaviors of leaders who have gone before you. Like any set of skills, leadership is developed by practice and repetition, over and over again, until you master it.

The rewards for becoming a leader are tremendous. As a leader, you earn the respect, esteem, and support of the people around you. You enjoy a greater sense of control and personal power in every part of your life. You become capable of achieving goals and objectives far beyond the ordinary.

The more you behave like a leader, the more positive you feel about yourself. You enjoy higher levels of self-esteem, self-respect, and personal pride. You feel stronger and smarter and more capable of getting results through others. You become more effective in bringing about positive changes in your work and personal life.

The Laws of Leadership have been identified and discussed over and over throughout the centuries. They are taught in military schools, colleges, and universities. They are taught in business schools and practiced every day in the businesses and organizations of our society. These laws and principles are followed by men and women everywhere who emerge to assume positions of power and authority whenever the situation demands it.

When you begin to think and act the way leaders do and you apply the Laws of Leadership to your life and work, you will attract to yourself opportunities to use more of your talents and abilities at ever-higher levels. The more you exercise the qualities of leadership in small matters, the more you will be given an opportunity to be a leader in larger matters. The better you fulfill your responsibilities today, right where you are, the greater the responsibilities that will be entrusted to you in the future. It is in your hands.

34. The Law of Integrity

—ᴍ—

Great business leadership is characterized by
honesty, truthfulness, and straight dealing
with every person, under all circumstances.

This law requires that you be impeccably honest with yourself
and others. As Emerson said, "Guard your integrity as a sacred
thing. Nothing is at last sacred but the integrity of your own
mind."

Integrity lies at the core of leadership, at the heart of the leader.
Everything you do revolves around the person you really are
inside. And the person you really are inside is always demonstrated
by your actions, the things you do and say.

Leadership has been defined as "the ability to get followers."
For people to follow you, to subordinate their interests to yours,
they must be able to believe in you and be willing to commit their
time, money, and energy to you.

Leadership is therefore a trust conferred upon you by others.
To earn this trust, to deserve this trust, you must be true to yourself. You must live in truth with yourself. Only then can you live
in truth with everyone else in your life and work.

Perhaps the most important thing you do as a leader is to be a
good role model. Lead by example. Walk the talk. Live the life.
Always carry yourself as though everyone is watching, even when
no one is watching.

Good leaders are completely reliable. People can take them at
their word and trust that they will do what they say. They make
promises carefully, and then they always keep their word.

A key mark of integrity in human relations is consistency, both
internal and external. The best leaders are consistent from one day
to the next, from one situation to the next. Because of this internal

consistency, these leaders are trusted. People know what to expect. There are no surprises.

Being consistent also means that you treat everyone the same. You do not have one persona for an important client and another for a subordinate. As Thomas Carlyle wrote, "You can tell a big person by the way he treats little people."

There are two basic types of leadership in business today, *transactional* and *transformational*. Transactional leadership is the ability to direct people, manage resources, and get the job done. But transformational leadership, the most important form of leadership today, is the ability to motivate, inspire, and bring people to higher levels of performance.

Transformational leadership is the ability to touch people emotionally, to empower them to be more and to contribute more than they ever have before. This ability enables transformational leaders to elicit extraordinary performance from ordinary people.

Leaders think about the future. They think long term. They think about how they want to be viewed by others, now and later in life. Because of this long time perspective, they never sacrifice their integrity or their reputations for short-term gain or profit.

There is a direct relationship between your feelings of self-confidence and self-esteem on the one hand and your levels of integrity and truthfulness on the other. The more you live your life according to your values, the better and happier you feel about yourself, no matter what happens around you.

How you can apply this law immediately:

1. Resolve to live in truth with yourself and with every person and situation in your life. Listen to your body and trust your intuition. Identify the main stress points and people problems in your life and then ask yourself, What is the right thing to do in this situation to resolve this problem and alleviate this stress?

2. Ask yourself: What kind of a company would my company be
   if everyone in it was just like me? What personal habits or
   behaviors would you need to change to answer this question
   in the affirmative? Whatever they are, do something today
   toward becoming the very best person you can be.

35. The Law of Courage

—ᴍ—

The ability to make decisions and act boldly
in the face of setbacks and adversity is the
key to greatness in leadership.

Winston Churchill once said, "Courage is rightly considered
the foremost of the virtues, for upon it, all others depend."

Leaders have the courage to make decisions and to take action
in the face of doubt and uncertainty, with no guarantees of success. Your ability to launch, to step out in faith, even when there
is a chance of loss or failure, is the mark of leadership. Leadership
is not lack of fear or absence of fear. Leadership is control of fear—
mastery of fear.

Everyone is afraid; leaders are simply those who face their fears
and take action in spite of their fears. And you develop the habit
of courage by acting courageously whenever courage is called for.

The natural reaction of most people is to avoid or to back away
from the things they fear. But when you force yourself to resist this
natural tendency and do the opposite, when you instead move
toward the thing you fear, your fear shrinks and loses its power
over you.

Glenn Ford, the actor, once said, "If you do not do the thing
you fear, then the fear controls your life."

The two greatest obstacles to success and personal effectiveness are the fear of *failure* and the fear of *criticism*. But every great success is preceded by many failures and accompanied by countless criticisms. It is the lessons you learn from these failures and your ability to rise above those criticisms that make your success possible in the long run.

Thomas J. Watson Sr., founder of IBM, once said, "If you want to be successful *faster*, you must double your rate of failure. Success lies on the far side of failure."

Make a habit of confronting your fears. If there is anything in your life that causes you anxiety, treat it as a personal challenge and resolve to deal with it. As Emerson wrote, "Do the thing you fear and the death of fear is certain."

The leader in any group or organization is the person who accepts the responsibility to turn and face whatever danger or threat is facing the group. Frederick the Great's motto was *"L'audace, l'audace et toujours l'audace!"* ("Audacity, audacity and always audacity!")

Audacity is often the best policy when decisions are demanded and action is necessary. Audacity may get you into trouble on occasion, but then, even more audacity will get you out. An old Zulu saying is "When faced with two dangers, one behind you and one in front of you, it is always better to go forward."

Resolve today to move out of your comfort zone, whatever it is. Great business success comes from taking risks, from going boldly where no one has ever gone before. Expand your envelope. Set what are called "BHAGs" (big hairy audacious goals) for yourself and your organization. Never be satisfied with the status quo.

Peter Drucker says, "Whenever you see a great business success, someone once took a big chance."

Remember, no matter how well you plan, your life will be a continuous succession of problems, difficulties, disappointments, setbacks, and obstacles that can easily discourage you and cause you to lose heart. The mark of a leader, however, is that the leader never allows himself or herself the luxury of discouragement or self-pity. The leader does not complain, make excuses, or wish that somehow things could be easier or different. Just keep reminding yourself, as Henry Ford once said, "Failure is merely an opportunity to more intelligently begin again."

Resolve today to develop the habit of courage by behaving courageously, by doing the things you fear, and by dealing boldly and straightforwardly with the difficult people and situations in your life. As Mark Twain wrote, "Courage is not lack of fear, absence of fear, but control of fear, mastery of fear."

How you can apply this law immediately:

1. Imagine that you could wave a magic wand and achieve any goal you set for yourself. What actions would you take in your business, what changes would you make, if you had no fear of failure at all? What goals would you set if you were guaranteed success? Whatever the answers to these questions, begin acting today as though your success were guaranteed.

2. Identify a specific fear in your life, such as public speaking or confronting others, that may be holding you back from realizing your full potential. Whatever it is, resolve today to deal with it and overcome it. As Dorothea Brande wrote, "Act as if it were impossible to fail, and it shall be!"

36. The Law of Realism

—ന—

Leaders deal with the world as it is, not as they wish it would be.

Your ability and your willingness to be completely *realistic* in your life and work are among the most important qualities of leadership. The measure of how realistic you really are is demonstrated by your willingness to deal straightforwardly with the truth of your life and business, whatever it may be.

Peter Drucker refers to this quality of realism in a leader as "intellectual honesty." Jack Welch, president of General Electric, calls it the "Reality Principle." He approaches every problem or difficulty with the question, What's the reality?

Concentrate on getting the facts. Facts don't lie. The more facts you gather, the better will be the picture of reality that you can develop. The quality of your decisions will be largely determined by the quality of the information on which those decisions are based.

As you gather the facts, discipline yourself to remain objective, to avoid jumping to conclusions. Seek the truth above all, rather than reinforcement or justification. Imagine, as an exercise, that this situation is happening to someone else and you have been called in as an outside observer to advise and comment. Standing back from a situation, or stepping outside of it, can give you a more honest and objective perspective that enables you to make better decisions.

One of the marks of "self-actualizing" people, according to Abraham Maslow, is that they are extremely honest and objective about themselves. They have no illusions. They are nondefensive and do not feel compelled to explain themselves to others. They accept themselves, as Oliver Cromwell said, "warts and all."

They know they are not perfect and they do not try to be. They do not feel it necessary to be someone they are not. They admit their weaknesses and adjust their behavior to compensate for them. They do not demand perfection of themselves and do not feel guilty when they make mistakes.

The fact is that most people, including very effective people, have more weaknesses than strengths. Organizations are built to maximize strengths and make weaknesses unimportant. Weaknesses are to be dealt with and compensated for, not avoided, rationalized away, or ignored.

Analyze yourself honestly. What are your greatest *strengths?* What are your areas of *weakness?* Your strengths are what have gotten you to where you are today. Your weaknesses are determining the speed at which you move ahead in your career. In what areas could your weaknesses be holding you back or limiting your effectiveness in your current situation?

Your weakest important skill sets the height at which you can use all of your other skills. The more honest you are with yourself and the more willing you are to deal straightforwardly with your life, the more effective you will be in dealing with the continually changing business situation around you.

What are the strengths and weaknesses in your *business* today? Ask questions continually, of everyone, to develop a better picture of your current reality. Read, study, attend courses, and get other viewpoints to build your picture of reality with greater clarity. Always be willing to face the weaknesses and imperfections in your company, whatever they are, and then resolve to do something about them.

If you are not happy with the way things are, think about the way you would like them to be and then get busy creating the reality you desire. Focus on the future rather than the past. Focus on the solution rather than the problem. Concentrate on where you are going rather than where you are coming from.

Refuse to allow yourself to get upset about things that have already happened and that cannot be changed. Something that has already happened is a fact. It is a part of reality. Sometimes the only thing that you can do about a fact is to control your attitude toward it. The way you react to an unalterable situation will often determine your effectiveness in the short term and your success in the long term.

Never trust to luck or hope that something unexpected will turn up to solve a problem or save a situation. Never allow yourself to wish, hope, or trust that anyone else will do it for you. You are the leader. You are in charge. Deal with your world as it is, not as you wish it would be.

How you can apply this law immediately:

1. Identify your major weaknesses, in terms of either personality traits or specific skills. What is your weakest personal quality? What is your weakest important skill? Whatever they are, identify them clearly and then make a plan to correct them.

2. Identify and analyze the realities of your company, your products, your services, and your methods of operation, as they are today. What are the weaknesses or areas of vulnerability in your business? Whatever they are, decide today to take some specific action to compensate for your weaknesses and to maximize your strengths.

37. The Law of Power

—m—

Power gravitates to the person who can use it most effectively to get the desired results.

Power is the ability to influence the allocation of people, money, and resources. It exists in all human relationships and situations. It is essential for the effective functioning of human life and society. It is neither good nor bad. It just is.

Power can be used in business in two ways: (1) to advance the interests of the organization or (2) to advance the interests of the individual. When power is used skillfully to advance the interests of the organization, it is a positive force. It can improve the situation of all the people who are affected by it.

If power is used, or abused, to advance the interests of the individual to the detriment of the organization, then power becomes a negative and destructive force that can harm the organization and the people in it.

Any given organization or system has a fixed quantity of power. If one person has more power, then another person will have less. All power struggles are aimed at getting a larger part of this fixed quantity of power.

The only way that the total amount of power can be increased is by increasing the size of the company, the quantity of activities, and the number of people in the organization.

The leader tends to be the person who is the most capable of seizing the reins of power and holding onto them. But ultimately, true and lasting power in an organization comes from the consent of the followers. Leaders become leaders and acquire power because other people want them to have that power. This is especially true in an open system where people are free to leave and take their support away if they are not satisfied with the way the power is being used.

The only way to keep power once you have acquired it is to prove yourself to be the most effective at getting results by utilizing that power.

Power is invariably the "power to do." What are you tasked to do with the power you have? When you demonstrate your ability to get results with the power you have, you will attract to yourself opportunities to expand your power. As your power expands, you will get more and more opportunities to get ever greater and more important results. Your power and influence will continue to grow as long as you demonstrate that you can deploy it more effectively than someone else.

Four Kinds of Power You Can Develop

There are four major types of power you can develop. The first is *expert power*. This is where you start. You concentrate on doing your job in an excellent fashion. When you are recognized as being very good at what you do, you acquire greater power and influence than people who are only average or mediocre. With expert power, you attract the respect and attention of the important people in your organization. You receive more opportunities to do what you do well. Doors open for you.

The second type of power you can develop is *personal power*. This form of power comes from being liked and respected by the people around you. The more people like you, the greater influence you have with them. People listen to you and are open to your suggestions and ideas. This type of power is often called "social intelligence" or "emotional intelligence." It is the most helpful and ultimately the highest paid ability in our society.

The third type of power, *position power*, is the power that goes with the job title. Position power includes the ability to hire and fire, to reward and punish. Position power can be separate from ability or personality. There are many unpleasant and incompetent people with position power who got it for reasons other than their ability to get the job done quickly and well or their ability to get along well with others.

Perhaps the best type of power, the fourth, is *ascribed power*. This is the power you have when the people around you willingly grant you authority and influence over them because of the person you are. You attract this power to yourself by being very good at what you do and, at the same time, by being liked and respected by the people around you.

Building a Power Structure

Power in business and society is based on a network of managed dependencies. A "dependency" is defined as someone who is willing to help you when you ask, even though you cannot order that person to do anything. Power is often dependent upon your ability to influence people over whom you have no direct control or authority.

You build a network of managed dependencies by continually looking for ways to help other people in some way—in advance. The more favors you do for others, without direct expectation of repayment, the more power and influence you acquire. The most powerful people in any organization or community seem to be those who have helped, or who can help, the greatest number of other people achieve their own goals and objectives.

How to Gain and Keep Power

The first step in acquiring power and influence is for you to become valuable, and then indispensable, to your organization. In the final analysis, results are all that matter. Keep yourself focused by always asking, What results are expected of me?

This is the starting point. The focus on results has always been the high road to personal power and greater influence. When you develop a reputation for doing your job well, you cannot help but be paid more and promoted faster.

The second step in securing your power is for you to make yourself more valuable and helpful to more and more people. Continually look for ways to go the extra mile, to do things that are beyond what others might expect.

The third way for you to expand your power is for you to continually seek opportunities to help and to add value both to your organization and to the people in it. Take additional courses, upgrade your knowledge and skills, and look for new ways to increase sales or cut costs.

Come to work a little earlier and stay a little later. Volunteer for additional responsibilities. Always do more than you are paid for and you will always end up being paid more than you are receiving today.

For you to acquire and keep power and influence, you will require supporters both inside and outside of your organization. You should give this subject a lot of thought. Who are, or could be, your most important supporters, and what can you do to strengthen your relationships with them?

Almost everyone in an organization has power of some kind. Everyone has the power to help or hurt in some way. Everyone has the power to do or to refrain from doing something that needs to be done. Each person is in a position to advance a cause or to hinder it, to help move things ahead or to block them. What are your powers in your organization? What are the powers of the people around you?

An important principle of power is that "power always arises to fill a vacuum." You can create power for yourself by stepping into a new and undefined situation where a power vacuum exists and assuming responsibility for results. You can acquire power in the most positive sense of the word by taking charge of a new project and committing yourself wholeheartedly to the success of the venture.

The more capable and competent you prove yourself to be at getting specific and important results for your organization, the more power, influence, and authority will flow to you, and the more valuable you will become.

How you can apply this law immediately:

1. Identify the individuals in your organization who have power of one kind or another—expert power, position power, personal power, or ascribed power. What are some of the things that you could do personally to develop your power in one or more of these areas?

2. Define the most important results expected of you in your position. How could you increase the quality and quantity of your results? Identify one thing that you could do differently right now to be more effective.

38. The Law of Ambition
—⚋—

Leaders have an intense desire to lead; they have a clear vision of a better future, which they are determined to realize.

Vision is the one common quality that separates leaders from nonleaders. Leaders have a clear picture of the kind of future they want to create, and they have the ability to communicate this vision to others in an exciting and inspiring way.

People may work steadily for a paycheck, but they will perform at high levels only when they are inspired by a vision of some kind. The development and articulation of this vision is a key responsibility of leadership.

Leaders have the ability to visualize, to see the big picture and then to inspire others to work together to make it a reality. The true leader sees leadership as a tool he or she can use to bring about a result that is bigger and more important than any single individual.

You become a leader when you set a goal, make a plan, and then throw your whole heart into making it a reality. You become a leader when you develop an inspiring vision for yourself and others. You become a leader when you know exactly where you want to go, why you want to get there, and what you have to do to achieve it.

Leaders can explain clearly to other people what it is they are trying to accomplish, why they are trying to accomplish it, and how they are going to bring it about. They are eager to get results and they are impatient with delays. They are excited about what they are doing, and as a result, they get other people excited as well.

Leaders have goals, plans, and strategies that they are working to implement every day. They are in a hurry. They have a lot to do and they feel that they have too little time.

Perhaps the most important part of ambition is *clarity* on the part of the leader. The leader has a clear vision, clear values, a clear mission, and clear, written goals, plans, and strategies for his or her department or organization.

Most of all, leaders want to lead, to be in charge, to be responsible, to make things happen. They are willing to endure the risks and the sacrifices that are required to make a real difference in their worlds.

The very act of setting clear goals for yourself and for your team moves you up in the ranks of leadership. It pushes you toward the front of the line. To be a leader, you must be leading others in a specific direction toward a specific goal for the accomplishment of a specific result. The clearer you are about your vision, your values, your mission, and your goals, the more effectively you will lead, guide, direct, and inspire others.

How you can apply this law immediately:

1. Determine a clear vision for yourself and your organization. Where would you ideally like to be in three to five years? Define it clearly. Write it down. Share it with others. The more clear and specific you are about your future vision for yourself and your company, the more you will accomplish and the better and more effective leader you will become.

2. Decide what it is that you really want to do with your life. This is the great question of leadership. If you had no limits whatsoever in terms of time, money, and resources, what would you be the most excited about achieving for yourself and your organization? Begin today to think in terms of how you can accomplish it, and then take action on it immediately.

39. The Law of Optimism
—∿—

The true leader radiates the confidence that
all difficulties can be overcome and all goals
can be attained.

Optimism in a leader inspires and empowers people to believe that they can do more and be better than they ever have before. It is one of the most powerful of all qualities for leadership and success in personal and business life. And you learn to become an optimist by practicing the behaviors of other positive, optimistic, future-oriented people.

You become an irrepressible optimist by practicing the habits of optimism whenever they are called for. Optimism is the foundation of a positive mental attitude. Optimism is the ability to find something worthwhile in every situation. It has been best defined as "a generally positive and constructive response to stress."

The only things you can control in your life are your responses to the inevitable problems and difficulties you face each day. How you respond to a situation, or how you interpret the situation, determines how you feel about it. Your feelings, your emotions, then determine the clarity and effectiveness of your thoughts and your responses. The more optimistic and positive you are, the calmer, more positive, and more creative you will be.

Optimists are "Can do!" people. They look for the good in every situation. When something goes wrong, they say, "That's good!" and then look for something that is good within the problem or difficulty. And they always find it.

Optimists seek the valuable lesson in every setback or disappointment. As Napoleon Hill wrote, "They look for the seed of an equal or greater benefit or advantage in every setback or obstacle." They operate on the principle that "Difficulties come not to obstruct, but to instruct."

Optimists focus on the future rather than the past. They look for the opportunity in every difficulty. They think about what can be done now rather than focusing on what has happened in the past and who is to blame for it.

Above all, optimists are *solution oriented* rather than problem oriented. They focus on the solution, on the next step, rather than the problem. They think in terms of what can be done now rather than what has happened or who is to blame.

You can change your mind from negative to positive in one second by taking your mind off the problem and focusing exclusively on the solution to whatever challenge is facing you. Make it a habit. Whenever you are faced with a problem of any kind, immediately stop and ask, Okay, what do we do now? What's the next step? Where do we go from here?

Imagine that your biggest problem, whatever it is, has been sent to you at this time to teach you something valuable that you need to learn. It is exactly what you need for your ongoing growth and development. It contains a gift of wisdom that has been designed just for you, at this moment in your life.

What could be the most important lesson or insight contained in the biggest problem or difficulty you are wrestling with today?

Thomas Edison became the greatest inventor in America and one of the richest people in the world by following a simple philosophy. He believed that success consisted of, first, defining the desired invention or product and then, second, experimenting until he had eliminated every way that would not work. Edison believed that success was merely a process of elimination, of repeated failures, of continuing to experiment until the correct method was found.

When you begin to look upon each temporary failure or setback as a stepping-stone on the road to the success that must inevitably come, you will become a completely optimistic, positive, highly creative, and effective person and leader.

How you can apply this law immediately:

1. List your three most important goals in life, right now. Then, write down one step that you can take immediately to move you in the direction of each of those goals. This simple exercise will give you an increased sense of control and personal power.

2. List your three biggest worries or concerns today. Decide on at least one specific action you can take in each case to begin solving the problem or resolving the worry or concern.

3. Identify the most valuable lesson that could be contained in the biggest single problem you are wrestling with right now. When you begin to identify and capitalize on the lessons contained in every difficulty you face, you will begin to move ahead at a more rapid rate than ever before.

40. The Law of Empathy

—⚏—

Leaders are sensitive to and aware of the needs, feelings, and motivations of those they lead.

Leaders have high levels of "interpersonal intelligence." They are constantly aware of the thoughts, feelings, and possible reactions of others to the things they do and say. They take time to think about the effects of their decisions on their people before they make them. They recognize that how people feel will largely determine how well they perform.

Leaders are good listeners. They listen carefully to what others say and they seek to understand what is being said between the lines. They are open to feedback from their people, and they are willing to change their decisions based on new information. They are flexible rather than rigid.

As a leader, you realize that different people require different things from each leadership situation. Sometimes, they require that you be clear and direct. Other times, they require that you be more relaxed and participatory. The required leadership behavior will vary from person to person and from situation to situation.

Leaders vary their approaches to people depending on what different people need to perform at their best. Leaders recognize that their own personal behaviors of consideration, courtesy, caring, and kindness toward their people are critical determinants of individual performance.

For people to perform at their best, they need to know exactly what is expected of them. Leaders take time to make job assignments and responsibilities clear. They make sure everyone knows exactly what he or she is expected to do, how important it is, and when it is supposed to be completed.

Everyone wants to feel good about himself or herself. Leaders continually look for ways to use praise, approval, and positive reinforcement to elicit the very best from their people.

Leaders continually create situations that empower people, that make people feel stronger and more confident. They lead by encouragement and commitment rather than by fear and threats.

Leaders encourage people to speak freely and openly about their real thoughts and concerns. They realize that the quality of a relationship between two people can be measured by how freely each feels to speak honestly to the other and to express their true opinions.

How you can apply this law immediately:

1. Make a list of the people who report to you and then consider the kind of direction and supervision they need from you to perform at their best. How could you adjust your leadership style to be more effective with each of them?

2. Be a good listener. Practice asking more questions of your people and then listening quietly and attentively to the answers. Remember that you do not need to comment or to reply to everything that people say. You only need to listen well.

3. Ask the people around you for their advice, ideas, and input. Encourage people to be open and direct with you. Think of how you could improve your relationships with your people by being more relaxed and receptive to the different ideas and viewpoints they might have.

41. The Law of Resilience

—⁓—

Leaders bounce back from the inevitable setbacks, disappointments, and temporary failures experienced in the attainment of any worthwhile goal.

The one thing that is inevitable in business and in leadership is the *crisis*. If you are actively involved in your life and your work, you will move in and out of crises on a regular basis. Your ability to respond effectively to a setback or crisis is the true mark of leadership, the true test.

When something goes wrong, everyone watches the leader to see how he or she is going to respond. The leader's behavior in a difficult situation sets the tone for the whole organization.

Life is a continuous succession of problems and difficulties. There is no success without temporary failure. Setbacks and disappointments are inevitable and unavoidable. Your ability to respond positively and constructively to adversity will prove how far you have come as a person. Keep reminding yourself, "It's not how far you fall, but how high you bounce, that counts!"

Your ability to solve problems and make the right decisions prior to taking action will determine your success as much as any other factor. When things go wrong, calm yourself, take a deep breath, and immediately begin gathering the facts of the situation so that you can make a good decision.

How you can apply this law immediately:

1. Identify the three worst things that could go wrong in your business life, your job, or your career. Develop a contingency plan for each one. Imagine that what *can* go wrong, *will* go wrong and begin making provisions against possible problems immediately.

2. Engage in "crisis anticipation" regularly, looking down the road and imagining the problems that could occur. Discuss the subject with others. Brainstorm different countermeasures you could take in the case of any eventuality.

3. Identify the major source of worry or stress in your life today. What is it? Now, ask, What is the worst possible outcome of this situation? Once you have determined the worst possible outcome, begin immediately to make sure that it does not happen.

42. The Law of Independence

—∿—

Leaders know who they are and what they believe in, and they think for themselves.

Leaders tend to be independent in their thinking. They are very clear about their values, their goals, and their personal missions. They are clear about what they stand for and believe in. They don't deviate from their values for any reason, especially the core values of integrity and responsibility.

Leaders have a reasonable concern for the feelings and opinions of others, but they are neither hypersensitive nor preoccupied with possible disapproval or disagreement. They invite input and ideas from others, but then they make their own decisions. They go their own ways.

Leaders tend to be nondefensive. They accept responsibility and refuse to make excuses. They don't rationalize, justify, or blame others. They don't get upset about criticism, disagreements, or unexpected reversals.

Leaders know their own strengths and weaknesses, and they accept them. As a result, they largely accept other people and do not try to change them. They avoid judging or condemning others. They accept that people are who they are and that they are not likely to change.

Above all, leaders set high standards for themselves and continually strive to live up to their own standards. They don't compare their character with others'. Instead, they compare themselves only against themselves and measure themselves against the very best that they can be personally.

Leaders have clear goals and objectives for themselves, and they work on their own schedules, at their own time, at their own pace. They look to themselves for the reasons for both their successes and their failures. They realize that they are not perfect, and they continually strive to improve in the important areas of their lives.

How you can apply this law immediately:

1. Decide for yourself what you really like and enjoy. What activities make you feel the very best about yourself? How could you organize your work so that you are doing more of these activities more often?

2. Be clear about your most important values and beliefs. Decide exactly what you believe in and what you stand for. Then make sure that everything you do is consistent with your highest values and your innermost convictions.

43. The Law of Emotional Maturity

—⚮—

Leaders are calm, cool, and controlled in the face of problems, difficulties, and adversity.

Emotional maturity is one of the most important and respected qualities of leadership. It requires, first, that you are at peace with yourself and, second, that you remain calm in the face of adversity and difficulty.

Emotional maturity enables you to live with uncertainty and ambiguity without becoming nervous or angry. Rather than fearing conflict or avoiding change, you accept them as essential and unavoidable parts of the leadership role. You embrace change and look for the opportunities that are contained in every change.

Leaders recognize that all you can do is your best. If a situation doesn't work out, then so be it. You do not go into fits of anger or recrimination when things go against you. You have a calm, healthy view of yourself. You can strive for higher goals and objectives, yet accept failure along the way.

Emotional maturity requires that you like and respect yourself. You have a positive self-image. You are able to endure the criticism and disapproval of other people without being bothered too much. You are able to do without either appreciation or rewards if they don't come immediately.

Emotionally mature people set their own standards and goals. They recognize that they are the only true judges of their own performance, no matter what anyone else says.

Emotionally mature people know when to make a decision and when not to. They have inner strength and personal security. They are predictable and steady.

Emotional maturity enables you to stay centered and balanced, to be calmer, more creative, and more effective in everything you do.

How you can apply this law immediately:

1. Think of the biggest challenges or difficulties facing you today. Ask questions to keep control, both of your emotions and of the situation. Some of the best questions are: What exactly has happened? What is the true situation? How did it occur? What do you think we should do? What is the next step?

2. Refuse to criticize, condemn, or complain, no matter what happens. Imagine that this difficult situation has been artificially created to test you, to see what you are truly made of. Act as if everyone is watching to see how you handle the problem and as if your future prospects are going to be determined by how calmly and relaxed you behave.

44. The Law of Superb Execution

—⚬—

Leaders are committed to excellent
performance of the business task at hand
and to continuous improvement.

A leader is the person who chooses *the area of excellence* for his or her team. A leader knows that excellence is a journey, not a destination. Leaders are committed to being the best in everything they do. They constantly strive to be better in their key result areas. They compare themselves with people, organizations, and products or services that are better than they are, and they are continually improving.

Leaders set standards of excellence for everyone who reports to them. They are ruthless about weeding out incompetence and poor performance. Leaders demand quality work and insist that people do their jobs well.

The leader sets the standard of excellence. No one, or no part of the organization, can be any better than the standard that the leader represents and enforces. For this reason, leaders are committed to personal excellence in everything they do.

Leaders are *learners*, continually striving to be better in their work and personal lives. They read, take additional courses and seminars, and listen to audio programs in their cars. They attend conventions and association meetings, go to the important sessions, and take good notes. They are committed to learning and growing in every area where they feel they can make an even more valuable contribution to their work.

People are most inspired when they feel that they are working for an organization in which excellence is expected. The very best way to motivate and inspire others is for you to announce your commitment to being the best in your field or industry. Then, continually benchmark your performance and the performance of your organization against the very "best in class" in your business.

Leaders identify their core competencies, the vital tasks they do that are responsible for them being in business. They continually look for ways to upgrade these core competencies to assure that they maintain a competitive edge in the marketplace.

Leaders think about the future and identify the core competencies that will be required for success in the years ahead. They then develop plans to acquire those core competencies well before they will be needed to compete effectively in the marketplace of tomorrow.

Above all, leaders think about *winning* all the time. They are committed to victory, to being the best in their chosen area. They are personally and emotionally bothered when they see their competitors doing well or better than they are in their businesses. They are continually looking for ways to improve and achieve superiority over other companies in their industry.

How you can apply this law immediately:

1. Identify your personal "area of excellence." What is it that you do exceptionally well that makes you uniquely valuable to your organization? What should it be? What could it be?

2. Identify your personal core competencies. What are the essential skills of your job, the abilities that make you valuable, if not indispensable? What core competencies do you need to acquire if you want to be the best in your field in the years ahead? Make a plan today to develop the key skills and core competencies you will need tomorrow.

45. The Law of Foresight

—⚶—

Leaders have the ability to predict and anticipate the future.

You should give a lot of thought to the future because that is where you are going to be spending the rest of your life. Your ability to accurately anticipate the future largely determines the success or failure of yourself and your organization.

Foresight is the ability to analyze the current situation and to accurately predict what is likely to happen as a result. The best leaders are those who continually look down the road and prepare carefully for possible reversals well in advance of them taking place.

Leaders know that potential successes have often been turned into disasters because of the failure of the leader to anticipate a setback in some area. Even if there is only a small probability that a serious problem or reversal could occur, you should seriously consider it and plan against it.

Leaders also have the ability to anticipate opportunities before anyone else sees them. They can then move quickly to assemble the resources necessary to take advantage of the situation when the opportunity presents itself.

How you can apply this law immediately:

1. Look into the future and imagine the most exciting opportunities that could occur for you in the next few years. How could you begin preparing today to take advantage of them?

2. Identify the greatest difficulties or reversals that could take place in the next one, two, or three years. What could you do today to make sure they don't happen?

Summary

Leaders are made, not born. They are usually self-made, as the result of long, hard work on themselves. And everyone has leadership qualities waiting to be developed.

Leadership emerges in response to situations that require the very best you have to offer. When you think like a leader and behave like a leader, when you accept the mantle of responsibility without making excuses, blaming, looking to others, or running for cover, you become the leader.

And the whole world opens up to you.

CHAPTER FIVE

The Laws of Money

—ᴍ—

46. The Law of Abundance

47. The Law of Exchange

48. The Law of Capital

49. The Law of Time Perspective

50. The Law of Saving

51. The Law of Conservation

52. Parkinson's Law

53. The Law of Three

54. The Law of Investing

55. The Law of Compound Interest

56. The Law of Accumulation

57. The Law of Magnetism

58. The Law of Accelerating Acceleration

The Laws of Money

—⋙—

One of your major goals in life should be financial independence. You must aim to reach the point where you have enough money so that you never have to worry about money again. The good news is that financial independence is easier to achieve today than it has ever been before. We live in the richest country at the richest time in all of human history. We are surrounded by more wealth and affluence than ever before. Your job is to get your fair share.

The Law of Cause and Effect applies to money as much as to any other subject. This law says that financial success is an effect. As such, it proceeds from certain, specific causes. When you identify these causes and implement them in your own life and activities, you will see the same effects that hundreds of thousands, and even millions, of others have seen. You can achieve whatever level of affluence you really want if you just do what others have done before you to achieve the same results. And if you don't, you won't. It is as simple as that.

There is perhaps no other area where universal laws are more in evidence than in the acquiring and keeping of money. In America today, there are several million men and women who started with nothing or deeply in debt and achieved financial independence. Their attitudes and behaviors have been studied in great depth. We now know the keys to wealth creation better than ever before. And what we know is that your most cherished beliefs on the subject of money will be the primary determinants of how much you acquire and how much you keep over the course of your working lifetime.

Your primary aim in life should be the achievement of your own happiness. However, happiness is something that exists naturally in the absence of fears, doubts, and negative emotions. One of the factors that most deprives you of happiness is worry about money. And, by the way, when we talk about money worries, we're not referring to your having *too much*. The problem is virtually always that people feel that they have *too little* money and their lives are suffering as a result.

Perhaps the greatest single fear, the one that causes you more distress and unhappiness than anything else, is the fear of failure. In the area of money, you experience this as the fear of poverty and the fear of loss. Since one of the deepest needs of humans is security, any threat to your security, real or imaginary, can cause you tremendous stress.

You can free yourself from the fears of poverty and failure only by achieving a specific level of financial worth and then by building a fortress around it so that it is safe and impregnable. This achievement of financial independence is a key responsibility of adult life. No one else will do it for you.

In psychology, money is what is called a "deficiency need." This means that it motivates you only when you feel deficient in it, when you feel that you don't have enough. Above a certain level, when you feel that you have enough, it is no longer a motivator. Put another way, when you have enough money, you don't think about it very much. But when you have too little, you think about it all the time.

The effect money has on your emotional life depends on your attitude toward it. If you feel that you have too little, money can become an obsession for you. It can dominate your thinking, feelings, and actions. Arguments over money are a major reason for marital breakdown. Problems with money are the primary reason for business collapse, the ruination of friendships, and psychosomatic illnesses of all kinds. It's not uncommon for people even to kill themselves over money problems.

The Reality Principle applies especially to matters of money. This principle states that "You must deal with life as it is, not as you wish it were or could be."

Most people live in a world of partial self-delusion, or even fantasy, with regard to money. They wish, hope, and pray about their financial futures while at the same time, deep in their hearts, they know their dreams will never materialize.

In Lewis Carroll's book *Alice in Wonderland,* one of the characters says happily that she is quite capable of believing several impossible things before breakfast each day. In the same way, many people believe quite impossible things about money, and then they wonder why they are having so many financial problems.

One of the most common obstacles to achieving financial independence is a deep-seated belief that somehow money is wrong and that people who have a lot of it are inherently evil. This belief is not based on any factual foundation. It goes back to early childhood conditioning when children are often told this because of other people's desire to rationalize away their own financial failures.

When my wife and I got married, her entire family attended the wedding, as did my employer, a man worth more than $500 million. All their lives, the members of my wife's family had been led to believe that poverty was a virtue and, by extension, financial success was somehow unclean or evil. They were astonished to find that my employer, the richest man that they had ever met or heard of in their lives, was devoutly religious, a solid family man, very low-keyed, polite, courteous, and charming. It took them months, and in some cases years, to readjust their thinking.

They had been told by their church and their friends that anyone with that kind of money must be evil and nasty.

Another great mental obstacle to financial success is that some people believe that they don't really *deserve* to be rich. They were raised with a steady drumbeat of destructive criticism, as I was, that has led them to conclude, at an unconscious level, that they don't really deserve to be successful and happy. The worst effect of negative experiences in childhood, which are all too common, is that when people actually do succeed as the result of hard, hard work, they feel guilty. These guilt feelings cause them to do things to get rid of the money, to throw it away. They spend it or invest it foolishly. They lend it, lose it, or give it away. They engage in self-sabotage in the form of overeating, excessive drinking, drug usage, marital infidelity, and often dramatic personality changes.

The fact is that money is good. It takes money to buy homes, cars, clothes, toys, food, and most of the good things in life. Money has an energy of its own, and it is largely attracted to people who treat it well. Money tends to flow toward people who can use it in the most productive ways to produce valuable goods and services and who can invest it to create employment and opportunities that benefit others. At the same time, money flows away from those who use it poorly or who spend it in nonproductive ways.

Money is very much like a lover. It must be courted and coaxed and flattered and treated with care and attention. It gravitates toward people who respect it and value it and are capable of doing worthwhile things with it. It flows through the fingers and flees from people who do not understand it or who do not take proper care of it.

Some people say that they are not very good with money. But being good with money is a skill that anyone can learn through practice. Usually, saying that one is not very good with money is merely an excuse or a rationalization of the fact that the person is not very successful or disciplined with money. The person has not learned how to acquire it or to hold on to it.

The starting point of accumulating money is for you to believe that you have an unlimited capacity to obtain all the money that you will ever need. Look upon yourself as a financial success just waiting for a place to happen.

Money is good. Money gives you choices and enables you to live your life the way you want to live it. Money opens doors for you that would have been closed in its absence. But just like with anything else, an obsession with money can be hurtful. If people become so preoccupied with money that they lose sight of the fact that money is merely a tool to be used to acquire happiness, then money becomes harmful.

The Bible says, "The love of money is the root of all evil." It doesn't say, "*Money* is the root of all evil." It says, "The *love* of money is the root of all evil." It is the preoccupation with money, to the exclusion of the really important things in life, that is the problem, not the money itself. Money is essential to our lives in society. It is also neutral. It is neither good nor bad. It is only the way that it is acquired and the uses to which it is put that determine whether it is helpful or hurtful.

46. The Law of Abundance

—⚹—

We live in an abundant universe in which
there is sufficient money for all who really
want it and are willing to obey the laws
governing its acquisition.

Plenty of money is available to you. There is no real shortage. You can have virtually all you really want and need. We live in a generous universe, and we are surrounded by blessings and opportunities to acquire all we truly desire. Your attitude toward either abundance or scarcity of money will have a major impact on whether or not you become rich.

The first corollary of the Law of Abundance is
People become wealthy because they decide to become wealthy.

People become wealthy because they believe they have the ability to become wealthy. Because they believe this completely, they act accordingly. They consistently take the necessary actions that turn their beliefs into realities. And you can always tell what your beliefs really are by looking at your actions. There is no other way.

The second corollary of this law is
People are poor because they have not yet decided to become rich.

In the book *The Instant Millionaire*, by Mark Fisher, the old millionaire asks the boy who has sought his advice about becoming a millionaire, "Why aren't you rich already?"

This is an important question to ask yourself. However you answer this question will reveal a lot about yourself. Your answers will expose your self-limiting beliefs, your doubts, your fears, your excuses, your rationalizations, and your justifications.

Why aren't you rich already? Write down all the reasons you can think of. Go over your answers one by one with someone who knows you well and ask for his or her opinion. You may be surprised to find that your reasons are mostly excuses that you have fallen in love with.

Whatever your reasons or excuses, you can now get rid of them. The world is full of thousands of people who have had far more difficulties to overcome than you could ever imagine, and they've gone on to be successful anyway. So can you.

How you can apply this law immediately:

1. Imagine that every experience you have ever had with money contained a special lesson that was designed just for you to help you to ultimately become financially independent. What are the most important lessons you have learned so far?

2. Analyze yourself honestly and determine your biggest block, your major self-limiting belief, that holds you back from becoming more successful financially. Resolve to act from now on as if this block no longer exists.

47. The Law of Exchange

—ɯ—

Money is the medium through which people exchange their labor in the production of goods and services for the goods and services of others.

Before there was money, there was barter. In barter, people exchange goods and services directly for goods and services without the medium of money. As civilization grew and barter became too clumsy, people found that they could exchange their goods and services for a medium like coins, which they could then exchange for the goods and services of others, thereby making the whole process more efficient. Today, we go to work and exchange our work for money, which we then use to purchase the results of the work of other people.

The first corollary of the Law of Exchange is

Money is a measure of the value that people place
on goods and services.

It is only what a person will pay that determines the value of
something. Goods and services do not have a value separate and
apart from what someone is willing to pay for them. All value is
therefore subjective and personal. It is based on the thoughts, feelings, attitudes, and opinions of the prospective purchaser at the
moment of the buying decision.

The second corollary of this law is

Your labor is viewed as a factor of production or a
cost by others.

We have a tendency to look upon the "sweat of our brow," or
our work, as something special because it is so intensely personal.
It comes from us and is an expression of what we are. However, as
far as others are concerned, our labor is just a cost. As intelligent
consumers, as employers or customers, we want the very most for
the very least, no matter whose labor is involved.

For this reason, you cannot place an objective value on your
own labor. It is only what other people are willing to pay for your
labor in a competitive market that determines what you earn and
what you are worth in financial terms.

The third corollary of this law is

The amount of money you earn is the measure of
the value that others place on your contribution.

The way the market for labor works is simple. You will always
be paid in direct proportion to three factors: (1) the work you do,
(2) how well you do it, and (3) the difficulty of replacing you.

How much you are paid will be in direct proportion to the
quantity and quality of your contribution in comparison with the

contributions of others, combined with the value that other people place on your contributions.

The fourth corollary of the Law of Exchange is
Money is an effect, not a cause.

Your work or contribution to the value of a product or a service is the cause, and the wage, salary, or payment that you receive is the effect. If you wish to increase the effect, you have to increase the cause.

The fifth corollary of the Law of Exchange is
To increase the amount of money you are getting out, you must increase the value of the work that you are putting in.

To earn more money, you must increase your knowledge, increase your skills, improve your work habits, work longer and harder, work more creatively, or do something that enables you to get greater leverage and results from your efforts. Sometimes you have to do all of these things together. The highest paid people in our society are those who are continually improving in one or more of these areas to add greater value to the work that they are doing.

How you can apply this law immediately:

1. Study your business carefully and determine exactly what it is that you do that contributes the greatest value to the price of the products or services that your company sells. How could you increase the value of your personal contribution?

2. Ask yourself each day, Why am I on the payroll? Make a list of your answers and share this list with your boss and coworkers. Ask them to comment on it and tell you what it is you do that they feel makes the greatest contribution to the organization.

48. The Law of Capital

—⁓—

Your most valuable asset, in terms of cash
flow, is your physical and mental capital, your
earning ability.

You may not even be aware that unless you are wealthy already,
your ability to work is the most valuable asset that you have. By
utilizing your earning ability to its fullest, you can bring thousands
of dollars each year into your life. By applying your earning ability to the production of valuable goods and services, you can generate sufficient money to pay for all the things that you want in
life. The amount of money that you are paid today is a direct measure of the extent to which you have developed your earning ability so far.

The first corollary of the Law of Capital is

Your most precious resource is your time.

Your time is really all you have to sell. How much time you put
in and how much of yourself you put into that time largely determine your earning ability. Poor time management is one of the
major reasons for poor productivity and underachievement in
every industry in America. It is the number one problem for both
managers and salespeople in every field.

For example, study after study over the years, going back to
1928, show that salespeople work only about 20 percent of the
time. The average salesperson spends approximately one and one-
half hours per day in face-to-face, direct selling activities with
prospects and customers. The rest of the time is spent in socializing, reading sales literature, making telephone calls, traveling, and
other largely unproductive uses of those precious hours and minutes during the course of the day.

Managers are no better. In a recent study, 95 percent of managers admitted that fully 50 percent of their working days are spent doing things that have absolutely nothing to do with the reasons they are on the payroll. And much of the remaining time is spent in areas of low productivity, doing things of low value.

The second corollary of the Law of Capital is
Time and money can be either spent or invested.

To a certain degree, your time and your money are interchangeable. If you spend them, they are gone forever. You cannot get them back. They become sunk costs in your life.

On the other hand, you can invest them, in which case you get a return on them that can go on and on. If you invest your time or money in becoming more knowledgeable and better skilled, you can increase your value. By increasing your ability to get results for yourself and others, you increase your earning ability, your personal cash flow, sometimes for your entire career.

One of the smartest things that you can do is to invest 3 percent of your income every month back into yourself on personal and professional development, on becoming better at the most important things you do. In fact, if you just invested as much in your *mind* each year as you do in your *car*, that alone could make you rich.

Invest one hour of your time reading in your field every day. Listen to audio programs in your car. Attend every course that can advance you in your career. Get personal and professional coaching to help you get the very best out of yourself.

Build your intellectual capital, your personal value, and your earning ability continually. This commitment to regular and continuous personal and professional development will pay off for you in greater measure than you can believe. It will save you months and years of hard work at lower levels of achievement and income. Your return on the investment of your time and money in yourself can be absolutely extraordinary.

The head of training for Motorola recently estimated that the company is getting thirty dollars back for every dollar it spends on training its people. This is said to be the highest payoff investment of time and money that the company can make. Other companies report similar returns on their investment in training their executives and staff.

For you, it is the same. Nothing will give you a bigger and better "bang" for your buck than reinvesting a part of your time and money into your capability to earn even more. All wealthy and successful Americans have learned this sooner or later, and all poor and unhappy Americans are still trying to figure it out.

The third corollary of the Law of Capital is
One of the best investments of your time and
money is to increase your earning ability.

The purpose of corporate strategic planning is to increase "return on equity," or ROE. This requires organizing and reorganizing corporate activities so that the company is earning a higher return on the capital invested in the organization. In your work life, your *personal* equity is your mental and emotional capital. Your job, then, is to earn the highest possible return on your human capital, to increase your "return on energy."

Just as a piece of productive machinery represents capital, you are also a form of mental and physical capital that can produce large quantities of goods and services if you are developed to your highest and best use. This way of viewing yourself must become a key part of your attitude throughout your work life.

How you can apply this law immediately:

1. Make a list of your output responsibilities, the work you do that represents accomplishments, not activities. Examine the

list and rank these tasks by priority, on the basis of the value of the work to your company.

2. Make a list of all the tasks you do, day in and day out. Take this list to your boss and ask him or her to rank your tasks in terms of how valuable he or she considers them to be. Then resolve to work on your most valuable tasks every minute of every day.

49. The Law of Time Perspective

—ᴍ—

The most successful people in any society are those who take the longest time period into consideration when making their day-to-day decisions.

This insight comes from the pioneering work on upward financial mobility in America conducted by Dr. Edward Banfield of Harvard University in the late 1950s and early 1960s. After studying many of the factors that were thought to contribute to individual financial success over the course of a person's lifetime, he concluded that there was one primary factor that took precedence over all the others. He called it "time perspective."

What Banfield found was that the higher a person rises in any society, the longer the time perspective or time horizon of that person. People at the highest social and economic levels make decisions and sacrifices that may not pay off for many years, sometimes not even in their own lifetimes. They "plant trees under which they will never sit."

An obvious example of someone with a long time perspective is the man or woman who spends ten or twelve years studying and interning to become a doctor. This person takes an extraordinarily long time to lay down the foundation for a lifetime career. And partially because we know how long it takes to become a doctor, we hold doctors in the highest esteem of any professional group. This respect for doctors tends to be true in virtually every society. We appreciate and admire the sacrifices that they have made in order to be able to practice a profession that is so important to so many of us. We recognize their long time perspectives.

People with long time perspectives are willing to pay the price of success for a long, long time before they achieve it. They think about the consequences of their choices and decisions in terms of what they might mean in five, ten, fifteen, and even twenty years from now.

People at the lowest levels of society have the shortest time perspectives. They focus primarily on immediate gratification and often engage in behaviors that are virtually guaranteed to lead to negative consequences in the long term. At the very bottom of the social ladder, you find hopeless alcoholics and drug addicts. These people think in terms of the next drink or the next fix. Their time perspective is often less than one hour.

You move up the ladder socially and financially the day that you begin thinking about what you are doing in terms of the possible long-term consequences of your actions. As you begin thinking longer term and organizing your life and priorities with your future goals and ambitions in mind, the quality of your decisions will improve and your life will become better almost immediately.

The first corollary of the Law of Time Perspective is
Delayed gratification is the key to financial success.

Your ability to practice self-mastery, self-control, and self-denial, to sacrifice in the short term so you can enjoy greater rewards in the long term, is the starting point of developing a long time perspective. This attitude is essential to financial achievement of any kind.

The second corollary of this law is
Self-discipline is the most important personal quality for assuring long-term success.

Self-discipline was defined by Elbert Hubbard many years ago as "The ability to make yourself do what you should do, when you should do it, whether you feel like it or not."

Herbert Gray, a businessman, spent eleven years searching for what he called "the common denominator of success." He studied thousands of successful people and finally concluded, "Successful people are those who make a habit of doing the things that unsuccessful people don't like to do."

And what are these things that unsuccessful people don't like to do? Well, they turn out to be the same things that successful people don't like to do either—like getting up earlier, working harder, and staying later—but successful people do them anyway. The reason? Successful people are more concerned with pleasing *results*. Unsuccessful people are more concerned with pleasing *methods*. Unsuccessful people prefer activities that are "tension relieving." Successful people pursue activities that are "goal achieving."

Your ability to pay the price of success, in advance, and to continue paying it until you achieve the goal you have set, is the true mark of a winning human being.

The third corollary of this law is
Sacrifice in the short term is the price you pay for security in the long term.

The key word here is "sacrifice." When you resist the temptation to do things that are fun and easy and instead discipline yourself to do the things that are hard and necessary, you develop in yourself the kind of character that virtually guarantees you a better life in the future.

When you continually invest your time and money in improving yourself rather than frittering them away in idle socializing or television watching, you are putting yourself on the side of the angels. You are virtually guaranteeing your future.

Parents who work hard and save their money so that their children will have an opportunity to get an excellent education are practicing a long time perspective. They are making decisions that can have an impact on their children for years into the future. They are putting their children onto the "up" escalator of life.

How you can apply this law immediately:

1. Practice a long time perspective in every area of your life, especially in your financial life but also with your family and your health. Think of where you would ideally like to be in five years and begin today to take steps in that direction.

2. Decide how much you want to have as an annual income when you retire and how much of an estate you will have to have to give you that kind of income. Make a plan to acquire that amount and begin working on it today.

50. The Law of Saving

—∞—

Financial freedom comes to people who save
10 percent or more of their income
throughout their lifetime.

One of the smartest things that you can ever do for yourself is to develop the habit of saving part of your salary, every single paycheck. Individuals, families, and even societies are stable and prosperous to the degree to which they have high savings rates. Savings today are what guarantee the security and the possibilities of tomorrow.

The first corollary of the Law of Saving comes from the book *The Richest Man in Babylon* by George Clason:
Pay yourself first.

Begin today to save 10 percent of your income, off the top, and never touch it. This is your fund for long-term financial accumulation and you should never use it for any reason except to assure your financial future.

It is sad but true, but if you simply save for a rainy day, you can be sure that it is going to start raining very soon. If you save with the intention of spending the money as soon as you need it, you are going to need it sooner than you realize.

If you want to buy a house or take a trip, set up another fund for that purpose. But your savings/investment account should be untouchable.

The remarkable thing is that when you pay yourself first and force yourself to live on the other 90 percent, you will soon become accustomed to it. You are a creature of habit. When you regularly put away 10 percent of your income, you will become comfortable living on the other 90 percent. Many people start by saving 10 percent of their income and then graduate to saving 15 percent, 20 percent, and even more. And their financial lives change dramatically as a result. So will yours.

The second corollary of the Law of Saving is
Take advantage of tax-deferred savings and investment plans.

Because of high and even multiple tax rates, money that is saved or invested without being taxed accumulates at a rate of

30 to 40 percent faster than money that is subject to taxation. Self-made millionaires, according to Dr. Thomas Stanley's book *The Millionaire Next Door,* are almost obsessive about accumulating their funds in assets such as real estate, self-owned businesses, and equities that increase in value without triggering tax liabilities.

Invest in company pension and retirement plans, 401(k) plans, IRAs (individual retirement accounts), Keogh plans, Roth IRAs, education investment accounts, stock option programs, and whatever else has been approved by the Internal Revenue Service for long-term financial accumulation. Make every dollar count!

How you can apply this law immediately:

1. Begin today to put away 10 percent of your income. Set up a special account for this purpose and treat your contributions to this account with the same respect that you do your rent or mortgage payments each month.

   If you are in debt and 10 percent is too much for you, start by saving 1 percent of your income and living on the other 99 percent. When you become comfortable living on 99 percent of your income, increase your savings rate to 2 percent. Over time, work the rate up to 10, 15, and even 20 percent of your income.

2. Become a lifelong student of money. Read the best books, take courses, and subscribe to the most helpful magazines. Know what you are doing so you can always make intelligent decisions when you invest your funds.

51. The Law of Conservation

—∞—

It's not how much you make but how much you keep that determines your financial future.

Many people make a lot of money in the course of their working lifetimes. Sometimes, during boom periods, people greatly exceed their expectations and make more money than they ever thought possible.

Unfortunately, they often develop the "walk on water" syndrome. They begin to believe that their success is because of their remarkable skills and abilities that they are using so well in a particular field. In many cases, it's just because the economy or that particular field is booming. They assume that because they are making a lot of money, they have the ability to go on making a lot more indefinitely. They then spend everything they earn, confident that they will always be able to earn more.

The true measure of how well you are *really* doing is how much you *keep* out of the amount that you earn. Successful people are fastidious about putting away chunks of money regularly and paying down debt during prosperous times so that they have reserves set aside when the economy or business turns downward.

How to apply this law immediately:

1. Calculate your true net worth as of today. Make a list of all your assets and value them at the amounts you could actually get for them if you had to turn them into cash quickly.

   Then, add up all your bills, credit card balances, and mortgages and subtract them from your assets to get your net dollar worth today.

2. Divide the number of years you have been working into your net worth. The result is the true amount you have actually earned each year after your costs of living. Are you happy with it? If not, start today to do something about it.

52. Parkinson's Law

—∞—

Expenses always rise to meet income.

Parkinson's Law is one of the best known and the most important laws of money and wealth accumulation. It was developed by English writer C. Northcote Parkinson many years ago, and it explains why most people retire poor.

This law says that no matter how much money people earn, they tend to spend the entire amount and a little bit more besides. Their expenses rise in lockstep with their incomes. Many people are earning today several times what they were earning at their first jobs. But somehow, they seem to need every single penny to maintain their current lifestyles. No matter how much they make, there never seems to be enough.

The first corollary of Parkinson's Law is

Financial independence comes from violating
Parkinson's Law.

Parkinson's Law explains the trap that most people fall into. This is the reason for debt, money worries, and financial frustration. It is only when you develop sufficient willpower to resist the powerful urge to spend everything you make that you begin to accumulate money and move ahead of the crowd.

The second corollary of Parkinson's Law is
If you allow your expenses to increase at a slower
rate than your income and you save or invest the
difference, you will become financially independent
in your working lifetime.

This is the key. I call it the "wedge." If you can drive a wedge
between your increasing earnings and the increasing costs of your
lifestyle, and then save and invest the difference, you can continue
to improve your lifestyle as you make more money. By consciously
violating Parkinson's Law, you will eventually become financially
independent.

How you can apply this law immediately:

1. Imagine that your financial life is like a failing company that
   you have taken over. Institute an immediate financial freeze.
   Halt all nonessential expenses. Draw up a budget of your fixed,
   unavoidable costs per month and resolve to limit your expenditures temporarily to these amounts.

   Carefully examine every expense. Question it as though
   you were analyzing someone else's expenses. Look for ways to
   economize or cut back. Aim for a minimum of a 10 percent
   reduction in your living costs over the next three months.

2. Resolve to save and invest 50 percent of any increase you
   receive in your income from any source. Learn to live on the
   rest. This still leaves you the other 50 percent to do with as you
   desire. Do this for the rest of your career.

53. The Law of Three

—ᘉ—

There are three legs to the stool of financial
freedom: savings, insurance, and investment.

One of your major responsibilities, to yourself and to the people who depend on you, is to build a financial fortress around yourself over the course of your working lifetime. Your job is to create an estate within which you can be safe from the financial insecurities experienced by most people. To achieve this goal, you need to maintain the correct proportions of your finances in each of these three areas: savings, insurance, and investment.

The first corollary of the Law of Three is

To be fully protected against the unexpected, you
require liquid savings equal to two to six months of
normal expenses.

Your first financial goal is to save enough money so that if you lost your source of income for up to six months, you would have enough put aside to carry you over. The very act of saving this amount of money and putting it into a high-yielding savings account or a money market account will give you a tremendous sense of confidence and inner peace. Knowing that you have this money put away will make you a far more effective human being than you would be if you were worried about your next paycheck and your next bag of groceries.

A young woman who attended one of my seminars, where we discussed the importance of saving money, wrote to me a year later and told me an interesting story. She said that she had never considered the fact that she was completely responsible for her own financial well-being. She had always spent everything she earned and a little bit more besides on her credit cards. As a result, she was always in debt.

From that seminar forward, however, she began saving some of her income from every paycheck, starting with 5 percent and increasing the amount over time. She became so good at saving that within a year she had almost two months of income put aside in her bank account.

Meanwhile, her company went through some changes and she ended up with a new boss. This manager turned out to be pushy, critical, and demanding. At first, she put up with his behavior. But then it dawned on her that she had enough money so that she could just walk away. And so she did.

She told me that this decision had changed the way she thought about herself and her life. Up to that time, she had been a bit passive and just accepted what her employers did and said. After that experience, she saw that having money in the bank put her in charge of her own life.

Financial reserves made it possible for her to quit doing something she no longer enjoyed and allowed her to take her time finding a better job at which she was paid substantially more. She wrote in her letter that if she had not started saving, she would have been trapped in her old job. She would have been unable to leave, and she would have lost her self-respect and self-confidence.

The second corollary of the Law of Three is
You must insure adequately to provide against any emergency that you cannot pay for out of your bank account.

Always take out insurance against an emergency that you cannot write a check to cover. Carry sufficient health insurance to provide for yourself and your family in any medical emergency. Insure your car for liability and collision. Insure your life so that if something unfortunate happens to you, the people who are counting on you will be provided for. Perhaps the deepest need or craving of human nature is the desire for security, and without adequate insurance, you are not secure. Often, you are taking risks that you simply cannot afford.

The third corollary of this law is
Your ultimate financial goal should be to accumulate capital until your investments are paying you more than you can earn on your job.

Your life is divided into roughly three parts, although these three parts tend to overlap. First, there are your *learning* years, where you grow up and get an education. Then there are your *earning* years, from approximately age twenty to age sixty-five. Finally come your *yearning* years, when you can retire, with the average life expectancy today approaching eighty years, and rising.

The simplest and most effective of all financial strategies is for you to save and invest your money throughout your working lifetime until your money is paying you more than you earn at your job. At that point, you can begin to phase out of your regular job and spend your time managing your assets. This seems like a very simple lifetime planning strategy, but it is remarkable how few people follow it and how many people end up at the age of sixty-five with very little put aside. The average retired American today has a total net worth of approximately $31,000 plus social security income. Don't let this happen to you.

How you can apply this law immediately:

1. Calculate how much it would cost you to maintain your current standard of living if your income were cut off completely. Resolve today to begin saving until you have two to six times this amount set aside. Make this a top priority.

2. Sit down with a general insurance agent and arrange to be fully insured in every key area of your life—health, automotive, home, and life. Be a creative pessimist and imagine the worst that could possibly occur. Don't take a chance. Be sure you are covered, no matter what happens.

3. Begin a monthly savings/investment program today, even if all you do is go to the bank and open a special financial accumulation account. Put a fixed amount into this account every month and watch it grow.

54. The Law of Investing

—ɷ—

Investigate before you invest.

This is one of the most important of all the laws of money. You should spend at least as much time studying a particular investment as you do earning the money to put into that particular investment.

Never let yourself be rushed into parting with money. You have worked too hard to earn it and taken too long to accumulate it. Investigate every aspect of the investment well before you make any commitment. Ask for full and complete disclosure of every detail. Demand honest, accurate, and adequate information on any investment of any kind. If you have any doubt or misgivings at all, you will probably be better off keeping your money in the bank or in a money market investment account than you would be speculating or taking the risk of losing it.

The first corollary of the Law of Investing is
The only thing easy about money is losing it.

It is hard to make money in a competitive market, but losing it is one of the easiest things you can ever do. A Japanese proverb says, "Making money is like digging with a nail, while losing money is like pouring water on the sand."

The second corollary of this law comes from the self-made billionaire Marvin Davis, who was asked about his rules for making money in an interview in *Forbes* magazine. He said that he has one simple rule and it is "Don't lose money."

He said that if there is a possibility that you will lose your money, don't part with it in the first place. This principle is so important that you should write it down and put it where you can see it. Read it and reread it over and over.

Think of your money as if it were a piece of your life. You have to exchange a certain number of hours, weeks, and even years of your time in order to generate a certain amount of money for savings or investment. That time is irreplaceable. It is a part of your precious life that is gone forever. If all you do is hold on to the money, rather than losing it, that alone can assure that you achieve financial security. Don't lose money.

The third corollary of the Law of Investing is
If you think you can afford to lose a little, you're going to end up losing a lot.

There is something about the attitude of people who feel that they have enough money that they can afford to risk losing a little. You remember the old saying "A fool and his money are soon parted." There's another saying: "When a man with experience meets a man with money, the man with the money is going to end up with the experience and the man with the experience is going to end up with the money."

Always ask yourself what would happen if you lost 100 percent of your money in a prospective investment. Could you handle that? If you could not, don't make the investment in the first place.

The fourth corollary of the Law of Investing is
Invest only with experts who have a proven track record of success with their own money.

I had dinner with a self-made millionaire in Portland, Oregon, recently. He started with nothing and had gradually worked and invested his way to a net worth of several million dollars. He had a simple philosophy: He would invest only with people who had been successful at making money in the past. As he moved up financially, he would invest only with people who were doing better than he was with their own money.

Because he was relatively wealthy, he was often approached by people selling investments of various kinds. He would always invite the salesperson to trade personal financial statements with him. If the salesperson would show him his or her personal financial statements, he would show the salesperson his. If the salesperson was doing better than he was with the investments being recommended, he would accept the advice and buy the investment. If he was doing better than the salesperson with his current investments, he would decline. Many of the people who approached him with investments, in fact most of them, were not doing particularly well at all. They would leave quietly and never come back.

Your aim is to invest only with people who have a successful track record with money. In this way, your risk is reduced considerably. Don't lose money. If ever you feel tempted, refer back to this rule and resolve to hold on to what you have.

How you can apply this law immediately:

1. Think back over the various financial mistakes you have made in your life. What did they have in common? What can you learn from them? Accurate diagnosis is half the cure.

2. Invest only in things that you fully understand and believe in. Take investment advice only from people who are financially successful from taking their own advice. Play it safe. It's better to hold onto your money rather than to take a chance of losing it, along with all the time it took you to earn it.

55. The Law of Compound Interest

—〰—

Investing your money carefully and allowing
it to grow at compound interest will
eventually make you rich.

Compound interest is considered one of the great miracles of all of human history and economics. Albert Einstein described it as the most powerful force in our society. When you let money accumulate at compound interest over a long enough period of time, it increases more than you can imagine.

You can use the Rule of 72 to determine how long it would take for your money to double at any rate of interest. Simply divide the interest rate into the number 72. For example, if you were receiving 8 percent interest on your investment, and you divided the number 72 by 8, you would get the number 9. This means that it would take you nine years to double your money at 8 percent interest.

It has been estimated that one dollar invested at 3 percent interest at the time of Christ would be worth half the money in the world today. If the money had been allowed to grow and double, and then double again, and then again, and again and again, it would be worth many trillions of dollars today.

The twenty-four dollars paid by the Dutch to the local Indians for Manhattan Island, had it been invested at 5 percent interest, would today be worth more than $2.2 billion. Compound interest is a powerful force in wealth building.

The first corollary of this law is
The key to compound interest is to put the money
away and never touch it.

Once you begin accumulating money and it begins to grow, you must never, never touch it or spend it for any reason. If you do, you lose the power of compound interest, and though you spend only a small amount today, you will be giving up what could be an enormous amount later on.

A secretary in New York received a divorce settlement of $5,000 in 1935. She took the entire amount to an experienced stockbroker who purchased a selection of good stocks for her. Over the years, this money grew, through good times and bad, at a compound rate of 12 to 15 percent. Today, this woman, now retired, is worth just over $22 million!

If you start early enough, invest consistently enough, never draw on your funds, and rely on the miracle of compound interest, it will make you rich. An average person earning an average income who invested $100 per month from age 21 to age 65 and who earned a compounded rate of 10 percent over that time would retire with a net worth of $1,118,000!

How you can apply this law immediately:

1. Begin a regular, monthly investment account and commit yourself to investing a fixed amount for the next five, ten, or even twenty years. Select a company with a family of mutual funds

and investment instruments, and keep your money working, month after month and year after year.

2. Continually look for ways to free up chunks of money that you can put away to grow with the power of compound interest. Make a decision to choose long-term financial independence over short-term pleasures.

56. The Law of Accumulation

—w—

Every great financial achievement is an accumulation of hundreds of small efforts and sacrifices that no one ever sees or appreciates.

The achievement of financial independence will require a tremendous number of small efforts on your part. To begin the process of accumulation, you must be disciplined and persistent. You must keep at it for a long, long time. Initially, you will see very little change or difference, but gradually, your efforts will begin to bear fruit. You will begin to pull ahead of your peers. Your finances will improve and your debts will disappear. Your bank account will grow and your whole life will improve.

The first corollary of the Law of Accumulation is

As your savings accumulate, you develop a momentum that moves you more rapidly toward your financial goals.

It is hard to get started on a program of financial accumulation, but once you do get started, you will find it easier and easier to continue. The "momentum principle" is one of the great success secrets. This principle says that it takes tremendous energy to overcome the initial inertia and resistance to financial accumulation and get started, but once started, it takes much less energy to keep moving.

If ever you lose your momentum and slow to a halt, you can find it extremely difficult to start up again. Momentum is one of the secrets of success that you must develop and maintain in everything you do.

The second corollary of the Law of Accumulation is
By the yard it's hard, but inch by inch, anything's a cinch.

When you begin thinking about saving 10 or 20 percent of your income, you will immediately think of all kinds of reasons why it is not possible. You may be mired in debt. You may be spending every single penny that you earn today just to keep afloat.

If you do find yourself in this situation, instead of saving 10 percent, begin saving just *1 percent* of your income in a special account that you refuse to touch. Begin putting your change into a large jar every evening when you come home. When the jar is full, take it to the bank and add it to your savings account. Whenever you get an extra sum of money from the sale of something or the repayment of an old debt or an unexpected bonus, instead of spending it, put it into your special account.

These small amounts will begin to add up at a rate that will surprise you. As you become comfortable with saving 1 percent, increase your savings rate to 2 percent, then 3 percent, then 4 percent and 5 percent, and so on. Within a year, you will find yourself getting out of debt and saving 10 percent, 15 percent, and even 20 percent of your income without it really affecting your lifestyle.

How you can apply this law immediately:

1. Decide upon your long-term financial goals and then resolve to work toward them one step at a time. The first steps are the hardest, and you must discipline yourself to avoid backsliding into old habits.

2. Practice the Law of Accumulation in other parts of your life as well. Resolve to master a subject one page at a time. Lose weight one ounce at a time. Learn a language one lesson at a time. The cumulative effect can be enormous.

57. The Law of Magnetism

—⚶—

The more money you save and accumulate,
the more money you attract into your life.

The Law of Magnetism has been written about for more than 5,000 years. It explains much about success and failure in every area of life, especially in the financial arena. Money goes where it is loved and respected. The more positive emotion you associate with your money, the more opportunities you will attract to acquire even more.

In the parable of the *talents,* which was also the name of the currency of the day, Jesus said, "To him who hath shall more be given. But to him who hath not, even that which he hath shall be taken away." The modern version of this parable is "The rich get richer and the poor get poorer."

The reason that people don't accumulate or attract money is largely because of their thinking. This explains why people can come to America from third world countries and, if their thinking is right, achieve wonderful things that were not possible in their native lands with their old ways of thinking. With a new mind-set, they start to attract people, ideas, opportunities, and resources into their lives. In a few years, they learn the language, start successful careers and businesses, and build great lives. Many of them become wealthy.

The first corollary of the Law of Magnetism as it applies to money is

A prosperity consciousness attracts money like iron filings to a magnet.

When I first read about the importance of developing a "prosperity consciousness," in my early twenties, I didn't really understand what it meant. A "prosperity consciousness" sounded good, but I didn't know how to develop it. Over the years, however, I've found that as you develop a positive and expectant attitude toward money and you begin believing in the Law of Abundance, your emotions somehow magnetize the money that you have already and you begin to attract even more money into your life.

That is why it is so important for you to start accumulating money, no matter what your situation. Put just a few coins into a piggy bank. Begin saving even a small amount of money. That money, magnetized by your emotions of desire and hope, will begin to attract more to you faster than you can imagine.

John D. Rockefeller started working as a clerk earning $3.75 per week. From this amount, he gave half to his church and saved fifty cents. It wasn't much, but it was a beginning. By the time he was fifty, he was perhaps the richest man in the world. Throughout his career, he attracted opportunity after opportunity until he virtually dominated the production and distribution of oil and fuel in the United States. And he started by saving fifty cents a week.

The second corollary of this law is

It takes money to make money.

When you practice the self-restraint and self-discipline necessary to break out of the cycle of spending everything you earn and a little bit more besides, you demonstrate to yourself and others that you are the kind of person who can be trusted with money.

When I applied for a loan and a line of credit for my business some years ago, the bank demanded collateral of five dollars in assets for every dollar that I wanted to borrow. I was astonished!

I learned later that this is the common ratio that banks demand from a person with no credit history. The fact that the borrower has saved and accumulated assets is proof that he or she can be trusted with money. Later, with experience, the bank will lend money with only one or two dollars of collateral for every dollar the borrower wants.

As you begin accumulating money, you begin to attract more money and more opportunities to earn more money. This is why it is so important that you start, even with a small amount. You'll be amazed at what happens and how much easier it becomes for you to attract even more money.

You become what you think about most of the time. The key question then is, What do you think about, and how do you think about it, most of the time?

Self-made millionaires spend twenty to thirty hours per month thinking about and studying their finances. They carefully plan and organize their accounts. They consider every investment and expenditure before they make it. As a result, they make better financial decisions than the person who thinks less and decides more on impulse.

How you can apply this law immediately:

1. Imagine that you are already a big financial success. Treat your money, your investments, and your expenditures as if you were a wealthy person who has earned that money as the result of having a very sharp financial mind.

2. Take time every day, every week, and every month to reflect on your financial situation and look for ways to deploy your finances more intelligently. The more time you take to think intelligently about your finances, the better decisions you will make and the more money you will have to think about.

58. The Law of Accelerating Acceleration

—⁂—

The faster you move toward financial freedom, the faster it moves toward you.

It often takes a long, long time for you to bring about a noticeable change in your financial condition. Old habits die hard. Changing your financial life is very much like changing the direction of a great ocean liner. You can do it only one degree at a time. However, once the changes are put into place, they begin to speed up and gather momentum as they move you toward your goals.

The first corollary of this law is
Nothing succeeds like success.

The more money you accumulate and the more success you achieve, the more and faster money and success seems to move toward you, from a variety of different directions.

All the people who are financially successful today have had the experience of working extremely hard, sometimes for years, before they got their first real opportunity. But after that, more and more opportunities flowed to them, from all directions. The major problem most successful people have is sorting out the opportunities that seem to come at them from everywhere. It will be the same for you.

The second corollary of the Law of Accelerating Acceleration is

Fully 80 percent of your success will come in the last 20 percent of the time you invest.

This is a remarkable discovery. Just think! You will achieve only about 20 percent of the total success possible for you in the first 80 percent of the time and money that you invest in an enterprise, a career, or a project. You will achieve the other 80 percent in the last 20 percent of the time and money that you invest.

Peter Lynch, the former manager of the Magellan Mutual Fund, one of the most successful mutual funds in history, said that the best investments he ever made were those that took a long time to come to fruition. He would often buy the stock of a company that did not increase in value for several years. Then it would suddenly increase and go up ten or twenty times in price. This strategy of picking stocks for the long term eventually made him one of the most successful and highest paid money managers in America.

How you can apply this law immediately:

1. Prove this principle for yourself, on paper. Double a penny every day for thirty days. On the first day you will have one cent. On the second day you will have two cents. On the third day you will have four cents, then eight cents, then sixteen cents, then thirty-two cents, and so on. By the thirtieth day you will have several million dollars.

However, on the twenty-ninth day, you will have only half of the amount that you will have on the thirtieth day. And on the twenty-eighth day you will have only one-quarter of what you will have on the thirtieth day. Never make the mistake of taking your money out of an investment too soon and giving up all of the great increase that is possible for you.

2. Identify those areas where you have invested an enormous amount of time and energy without seeing a significant return. Examine each of these commitments carefully to see whether or not you might be on the verge of a major breakthrough.

Summary

The Laws of Money explain how you can achieve financial independence. No matter where you are starting from, even deeply in debt or working for someone else, you can make a start. Even if you haven't been serious about money in the past, you can start today to save your money, invest it carefully, get out of debt, and achieve your financial goals in life. Hundreds of thousands, even millions, of men and women have started from nothing and have become financially independent by following the laws and principles that you have just learned.

The only real question you need to ask with regard to money is, How badly do you want it? Remember that you are always free to choose. You are responsible. No one will do it for you. It is always up to you.

When you follow these laws and principles, and if you persist long enough and hard enough, nothing can stop you from achieving great financial success.

CHAPTER SIX

The Laws of Selling

—⚹—

The Laws of Selling

We all make our livings selling something to someone. Everyone works on commission. All of us are paid both tangibly and intangibly, on the basis of how well we sell ourselves, our ideas, and our products and services to others. It is not a matter of whether you sell or not, it is only a matter of how good you are at it.

Parents are continually selling values, attitudes, and behaviors to their children, and their children will grow up straight and strong to the degree to which the parents have sold them well. The very best leaders and managers are invariably described as excellent low-pressure salespeople. Since people do not like to be told, taught, or talked down to, the most successful human relations experts are those who can present their ideas in such a way that other people will embrace them as their own. As Dwight D. Eisenhower once said, "The art of leadership is getting people to do what you want them to do and to think of it as their own idea."

In business and industry, and in most organizations, you are paid based on your ability to sell the quality of your work to the people whose opinion is most important in determining your success. Those people who market themselves the most effectively move ahead far more rapidly in their careers than others who do not, even though they may not be more talented and they may not be producing more or better work. It's all in the selling.

Many people are uneasy about the word "selling," including many salespeople. But the fact is that the ability to persuade and influence others is central to a happy life. If you cannot influence and persuade others to your point of view, you run the risk of being ignored and viewed as unimportant to your organization. People who cannot present their ideas or sell themselves effectively have very little influence and are not highly respected. On the other hand, people who are persuasive and convincing in their arguments are often some of the most respected and successful people in our society.

The ability to sell well is one of the rarest talents in America. Top salespeople are some of the highest paid, most respected, and most secure of all professionals. It doesn't matter if you are a customer, a manager, a salesperson, or anyone else; you owe it to yourself to become excellent at selling whatever it is you sell to other people.

To speak specifically of the sales profession, according to the Pareto Principle, the "80/20 Rule," the top 20 percent of salespeople make 80 percent of the sales and earn 80 percent of the money. Research shows that the top 10 percent of salespeople open 80 percent of the new accounts and are some of the highest paid people in the world of business. If you are in sales, your job is to do whatever it takes, to work whatever hours are required, to overcome whatever limitations you may face, to join the top 10 percent. At that level of selling, your future is assured.

Wonderfully enough, more knowledge is available today than ever before on how to sell more effectively. The sales process has been carefully studied from every angle. Tens of thousands of sales conversations have been videotaped, audio taped, and personally monitored to find out exactly what it is that the very best salespeople do that enables them to be so successful. Today we know more than ever before about how you can succeed in selling, and that is what we will discuss in this chapter.

Selling involves three essential factors. The first is the product or service. The second is the salesperson. The third factor is the customer. All three must be properly suited to each other for a sale to take place.

The product or service must be right for the customer, but it also must be right for the salesperson if he or she is going to sell it to the customer. Some salespeople are excellent at selling one type of product or service and some salespeople are excellent at another. This compatibility has little to do with the product or service itself. It has more to do with the temperament, personality, values, and attitude of the salesperson.

It is hard, if not impossible, to sell something that you do not believe in and cannot commit to wholeheartedly. Many salespeople have found that by changing the types of products or services they are selling, they have gone to the top of their industries, whereas before they were merely wasting time. The starting point of sales success, then, is to make sure that these three factors are in place. Be sure that what you're selling is the right product or service for you to be selling to the right customer, the kind of customer you enjoy working with.

The product must be appropriate, the salesperson must be prepared, and the customer must need the product, want it, and be able to use it and afford it. If all of these ingredients are in place, successful sales take place one after another.

Several laws of selling explain all great sales successes and most sales failures. As you learn and apply these laws to your sales activities, you will make more sales than perhaps you ever thought possible.

59. The Law of Sales

—m—

Nothing happens until a sale takes place.

These immortal words come from the great salesman and sales trainer Red Motley. It is the sale that initiates the entire production process. It activates businesses and factories, provides jobs for the employees, pays salaries and wages, pays taxes and dividends, and determines the entire direction of society.

Whenever sales are good in any country or state, the economy is strong and full of opportunities for growth and prosperity. Whenever sales slow down, the economy begins to suffer, jobs are lost, and the prospects for the future diminish. Sales are everything!

The first corollary of the Law of Sales is
Products and services are sold, not bought.

No matter how good a product or service may be, in a competitive market and with customers who are busy and preoccupied with many other things, products and services must ultimately be sold. Someone has to sell them. The ability to sell is therefore essential for the survival and success of any business.

The second corollary of this law is
Customers need to be asked to buy.

No matter how much a customer likes you or your product, there is always a certain amount of indecision or hesitation at the point of buying. This indecision can stop the sale if you don't handle it effectively. The job of the professional salesperson is to help the customer through this difficult moment and into the buying decision. This ability to get the customer to take action is vital to the entire sales process.

The third corollary of the Law of Sales is
Eighty percent of sales are closed after the fifth
call or after the fifth closing attempt.

In complex sales, those involving more than one decision maker and more than one meeting with the client, most buying decisions are made after the fifth meeting or interaction with the customer. In simple sales, those requiring only a single meeting with the client or customer, most sales are closed after the fifth time that the salesperson asks a customer to make a buying decision. It is therefore essential that the salesperson plan the closing part of the sales conversation in advance and be prepared to ask for the order in a variety of different ways.

Corollary number four of this law is
Fifty percent of salespeople quit after the first call in a complex sale, and 50 percent of salespeople fail to ask for the order even once in a simple sale.

One of my clients, a national sales organization, sent consultants out to observe the company's salespeople in action with their customers. They found that the salespeople, well trained and professional, were asking for the order or inviting the customer to buy an average of four times per sales conversation. For a variety of reasons, their sales were not very high. They then taught their salespeople to ask for the order just one more time on average, or at least five times in each sales conversation. The results were immediate! Their overall sales doubled within the next thirty days.

Sometimes you are only one question away from a successful sale. Each time you ask a customer to give you an opinion or to make a commitment of some kind, the customer moves one step closer to making the final decision. Sadly enough, many salespeople quit when the sale is just within reach, by failing to ask one more time.

The fifth corollary of the Law of Sales comes from the New Testament teaching that says
Ask and ye shall receive.

There is no miracle to becoming a successful salesperson. Top salespeople see more people and ask more often. If you want to join the top ranks of sales professionals in your field, you must simply increase your frequency of contact with your customers, and then ask them to buy more often.

One of my clients, a billion-dollar company in California, paid thousands of dollars to bring in an outside consulting firm to find out why its sales were down. The consultants analyzed the sales activity of the sales force and found that, for a variety of reasons, the average salesperson was making only four customer contacts per week.

Based on these findings, and with no other changes, the company immediately instituted a contact management system that required each salesperson to meet, face-to-face, with at least two prospects per day, ten prospects per week. Companywide sales jumped 50 percent in the following month and continued to rise thereafter. This proved again that no amount of training or skill can replace the need to get face-to-face with prospects and customers.

How you can apply this law immediately:

1. Organize your selling activities in such a way that you are seeing more qualified prospects each day. The quality of customers is usually a function of the quantity of prospects. Get yourself or your salespeople in front of more people and, all other things being equal, your sales will increase.

2. Design your sales process and presentation in such a way that you are either asking for business more often or you are offering your prospects more opportunities to buy in each sales conversation. Often, you are only one question away from the order.

60. The Law of Determination

—ɯ—

How high you rise is largely determined by how high you want to climb.

How far you go in your field, how much money you earn, is not determined by *external* factors, by what is happening outside and around you. It is largely determined by *internal* factors, by what is going on inside of you. Your own personal level of desire and ambition more often determines your sales and your income than any other factor.

There are few limitations to how far you can go in professional selling. The field is wide open to you. You are the one who decides, and you are earning today exactly the amount that you have decided to earn.

The first corollary of the Law of Determination is

You must commit to being the best in your field.

The commitment to excellence in your field of selling, more than any other single decision, will assure you of great success. This commitment will propel you onward and upward. It will motivate and inspire you. It will keep you going in the face of discouragement and disappointment. All top salespeople got to the top only after they had made a firm decision to become the best at what they were doing.

The second corollary of this law is

To achieve high sales goals, you have to set them in the first place.

The starting point of great success in selling is to decide how much you want to earn each year and then to decide how much you are going to have to sell in order to earn that amount.

Break down your annual sales and income goals into monthly goals, weekly goals, and even daily goals. Divide your annual income goal by the number 250, which represents the number of working days in an average year, to determine how much you want to earn each day.

Then divide your daily earnings goal by eight hours to determine how much you want to earn per hour. Once you have determined your desired hourly rate, from that moment forward, do only those tasks that will pay you that amount. Do not do anything that does not pay you the amount you want to earn.

For example, if you wanted to earn $50,000 per year, dividing that number by 250 would give you $200 per day. When you divide $200 by eight hours, you arrive at $25 per hour. This is your desired hourly rate. If you earn $25 per hour, eight hours per day, 250 days per year, you will hit your target of $50,000 for the year.

From this moment onward, refuse to do anything that you would not pay someone *else* $25 per hour to do. Do not drop off your dry cleaning, wash your car, make your own photocopies, or phone your friends or family. These activities do not pay $25 per hour. Be strict with yourself. Practice self-discipline every moment. Use your time carefully hour by hour, throughout the working day. Do only those things that can pay you your desired hourly rate.

The third corollary of the Law of Determination is
You can't fly with the eagles if you continue to
scratch with the turkeys.

This observation comes from motivational speaker Zig Ziglar, and it says that in order for you to be one of the best people in your field, you must associate with the best people in your field. You must avoid the 80 percent of salespeople who are going nowhere.

Birds of a feather do flock together, and if you associate with negative people, you tend to become like them.

Most top salespeople tend to be "loners" in that they find, in order to keep themselves positive, motivated, and focused on their work, they must stay away from other salespeople who are not as motivated and as focused as they are. You must also discipline yourself in the same way. If you want to be a top salesperson, you must be around other top salespeople.

How you can apply this law immediately:

1. Decide right now that you are going to be among the very best in your field. Decide to join the top 10 percent. Determine exactly how much the top 10 percent of salespeople both sell and earn, and then set that number as your goal or target for the year. From that moment forward, resolve to do only those things that will get you into the top 10 percent. Do only those things all day long that pay you the kind of money you want to earn.

2. Get away from people who do not share your commitment to excellence. Associate only with the very best and most respected sales professionals in your company and your industry. Your choice of companions will largely determine your future. Choose carefully!

61. The Law of Need

—∿—

Every decision to purchase a product or
service is an attempt to satisfy a need or
relieve a dissatisfaction of some kind.

Every buying decision is an attempt to solve a problem or achieve a goal. One of the most important things you do in successful selling is to put yourself in the shoes of your prospect and see your offering through his or her eyes. You must determine what this product or service means to your prospect in terms of his or her goals or problems before you can offer it or sell it effectively.

The first corollary of the Law of Need is
Before selling anything to anyone, the salesperson must be clear about the need he or she is attempting to satisfy.

Top salespeople are skilled at asking good questions and listening carefully to the answers. This enables them to focus on satisfying the most important and pressing needs of the customer with their product or service.

The second corollary of the Law of Need is
Sales success comes from fulfilling existing needs, not creating new ones.

Your job is to uncover the needs that already exist, not to attempt to convince people that they have needs that they may not have thought of in the first place. What are they already doing or buying? How could you present your product or service as an improvement on that? Find out where it hurts and offer to take away the pain better than anyone else.

The third corollary of the Law of Need is
The more basic the need, the more basic the sales presentation.

If you are selling potatoes, which cater to the need for food, you can sell them simply by size and weight. Your sales appeal will be to appetite and attractiveness. Your basis of comparison with other foodstuffs will be simple and straightforward.

Corollary number four of this law, the flip side of corollary number three, is

The more complex the need, the more sophisticated and subtle must be the sales presentation.

For example, if you are selling perfume to women, your advertising and sales approach must be indirect and low-keyed. Perfume is a sensitive subject, used delicately, and is bought only when the salesperson can structure the appeal in such a way that it connects with the deep inner needs of the customer for beauty and self-realization.

Corollary number five of the Law of Need is

The obvious need is often not the real need for which the product will be purchased.

Never assume that you know the customer's real need. Each customer is different. The need that causes one customer to buy may not be the same for another customer. If you address the wrong need for this particular customer, no matter how good your product or service is, you will not make the sale. The very best salespeople are those who are the most sensitive and attentive to their customers. They do not even begin to attempt to sell until they are absolutely clear what it is that the customer is really interested in buying.

How you can apply this law immediately:

1. Define clearly the real needs of your customers that your products or services satisfy. Question your assumptions. Look beyond the obvious benefits and satisfactions your products offer to the subtler but often more important needs.

2. Look into the future and identify the needs that your customers have today that you are not satisfying. What modifications could you make to your offerings to satisfy even more

needs for your customers? What new products or services could you develop to satisfy the needs of your customers?

62. The Law of Problems

—m—

Every product or service can be viewed as the solution to a problem or the resolution of an uncertainty.

As a salesperson, you are basically a professional problem solver. You seek out people who have the particular problem that your product or service can solve. You are looking for prospects who can achieve their goals or resolve their uncertainties by means of your product or service. The more accurate you are about the most important problems your product or service will solve, the easier it is for you to both find more prospects and sell to them.

The first corollary of the Law of Problems is

Customers buy solutions, not products or services.

People don't care about you or what you sell. They care about themselves and their problems. A businessperson is interested in improving sales or productivity, decreasing costs, and increasing bottom-line profits. The businessperson does not care if you are selling hula hoops or mainframe computers. The businessperson is interested in his or her problem or need and a possible solution to it, not your product or service or your desire to sell it. When you begin to perceive yourself as a professional problem solver rather than a salesperson, your sales will increase immediately.

The second corollary of the Law of Problems is

The more pressing the problem or need, the less
price sensitive the customer and the easier the sale.

If a prospect has an intense need or desire for what you are selling, her concern about the price drops immediately. When a
prospect feels that he can clearly benefit from purchasing your
product or service, his desire to own it will often overwhelm his
concerns about price. If a person is really hungry, that person will
pay a lot to eat. Your job in the sales conversation is to increase the
level of the customer's desire for the benefits and enjoyment of
your product or service to the point where the price is not a major
obstacle to proceeding.

The very best salespeople are those who can show customers
how much better off they will be immediately with the product or
service. Focusing on the value of what you're offering is one of the
most powerful of all ways to reduce price resistance.

How you can apply this law immediately:

1. Think about how you could position or present your product
   in such a way that your prospects will see a clear and pressing
   need to acquire it and use it. What are your most satisfied customers already telling you about how they are benefiting from
   what you have sold them?

2. Present and explain your product or service in such a way that
   the value to your customers is so high and immediate that they
   will want to purchase it now, with far less concern about the
   price.

63. The Law of Persuasion

—∞—

The purpose of the selling process is to convince customers that they will be better off with the product than they would be with the money necessary to buy the product.

When you make sales presentations, you are asking customers to engage in a trade. You are telling customers that if they give you their money, you will give them a product or service in return that will be of greater value to them than the money they pay. In addition, it will be of greater value than anything else that they could buy with that same amount of money at the same time.

Remember the Law of the Excluded Alternative *(Every choice implies a rejection)*. When you ask customers to buy from you and to give you a part of their limited amount of money, you are asking them to forgo all other purchases and satisfactions that are available to them with the same amount of money at the same time. This is asking a lot.

The first corollary of the Law of Persuasion is

The customer always acts to satisfy the greatest number of unmet needs in the very best way at the lowest possible price.

A major part of your job is to demonstrate that customers will get more of what they want faster by purchasing your product or service than they would get if they bought something else.

The second corollary of the Law of Persuasion is
Proof that other people similar to the customer
have purchased the product builds credibility,
lowers resistance, and increases sales.

Every bit of information that you can present showing the customer that other people, similar to the customer, have already wrestled with this buying decision, have decided to purchase, and have been happy as a result moves you closer to making the sale.

One of the most powerful of all persuasion techniques in our society is called "social proof." We are all influenced by what others have done or are doing. We are much more open to buying a product or service when we know that other people like us have already bought it and are happy with it.

The third corollary of the Law of Persuasion is
Testimonials of any kind increase desirability and
lower price resistance to a product or service.

Testimonial letters or photographs of happy customers using and enjoying your product or service, or lists of satisfied customers, are powerful influence factors in persuading a person to buy. You should persistently solicit testimonials from your customers. Acquire them from every source possible and in every way you possibly can.

Testimonials can make your sales work much easier. You will find that almost all top salespeople use testimonials that praise and support the product or services they are selling and that are relevant to the customer they are selling to.

How you can apply this law immediately:

1. Think about how you can present your offerings in such a way that prospects perceive what you are selling as the fastest and

easiest way for them to get the specific benefits your product
or service offers.

2. Gather testimonials of every kind from every satisfied customer you possibly can. Build your sales presentation and your
sales materials around these testimonials. Continually prove to
your prospects that other people, just like them, are happily
using what you sell.

64. The Law of Security

—◊◊◊—

The deepest craving of human nature is the
desire for personal, financial, and emotional
security.

This explains one of the most powerful of all motivations for
the purchase of many products and services. An appeal to the need
for security of some kind can be persuasive enough to overcome
all concerns about price, timing, or inconvenience.

The first corollary of the Law of Security is

The survival instinct is the strongest drive in human
behavior.

Not only are we strongly motivated to make decisions that will
assure our own survival, but we are even more strongly motivated
to make decisions that will assure the survival and well-being of
our loved ones. Whenever you can present a product or service in
such a way that it offers to increase the likelihood of the survival
of the individual or a member of his or her family, you can make
a strong appeal to this key buying emotion.

The second corollary of the Law of Security is
The need for safety is a powerful motivator of
human behavior.

Safety is not quite as powerful a need as the need for survival, but it is very close. Sometimes, an appeal to greater safety will be stronger than an appeal to comfort or beauty or any other form of enjoyment. The industries of security systems, safes, locks, and alarms are built on this need for greater safety.

The third corollary of the Law of Security is
The need to increase certainty underlies much of
customer behavior.

Because safety and security are so important to mental and emotional well-being, customers are continually looking for ways to increase their level of certainty and lower their levels of risk.

For example, the fact that a company has been in existence for a long time assures the customer that dealing with it is safer than dealing with a younger company. An established track record of any kind increases the feeling of certainty in the mind of the customer. When you are selling, it is very helpful to tell your customer how long you have been in the business of offering that type of product or service. This kind of information is very comforting to a prospective purchaser. It makes you appear to be a safer choice when it comes to purchasing what you are selling.

How you can apply this law immediately:

1. Position yourself and your products as the safest choice in your industry. Rather than attempting to sell on the basis of lower price, focus instead on the greater degree of certainty your customers will enjoy when they buy from you.

2. Position your lower priced competitors as higher risk choices for prospective customers. Show that dealing with someone

else is more dangerous than dealing with you. Demonstrate that buying an alternate product decreases the level of certainty and comfort customers enjoy when they deal with you. Guarantees and assurances of quality go a long way in this regard.

65. The Law of Risk

—◇◇◇—

Risk is inherent in any investment of time, money, or emotion.

Risk is an unavoidable and inescapable fact of life. We are always acting, in every way possible, to reduce risk. This is the entire purpose, for example, of the insurance industry. Insurance is simply a way of pooling risks by taking premiums from a large number of people in order to cover the losses that will be suffered by a small number of them. In every purchase decision, customers are seeking every way possible to reduce the risk and uncertainty involved in buying anything from anyone.

The first corollary of the Law of Risk is

You are successful in sales to the exact degree to which you can position yourself as the low risk provider of your product or service.

This is one of the most important concepts in selling and an idea that you must build into all your sales efforts. Once customers have decided that they want to purchase the product or service that you sell, that doesn't mean you've made a sale. You must then convince them that of all the suppliers of your product or service, customers will enjoy the highest degree of security and certainty, and the lowest degree of risk, if they buy it from you.

Often the reason that you don't close a sale is because the customer doesn't feel secure in your promises concerning the use, enjoyment, or follow-up service and maintenance of your product or service. Convincing the customer that this is a safe decision is one of your most important tasks.

Corollary number two of the Law of Risk is

The primary obstacle to buying anything is the fear of failure, the fear of making a mistake in the buying decision.

The fear of failure is one of the most powerful of all blocks to human action. The fear of making a buying mistake is rooted in previous experiences. Perhaps the customer bought a product that didn't work or purchased a product or service that ended up costing too much. The customer might have bought something that invoked criticism or ridicule. The customer may have bought a product that broke and couldn't be repaired.

Everyone has had bad buying experiences. As a result, everyone is conditioned to be cautious and fearful about having those experiences again. This fear of failure is a major obstacle that you must overcome before you can sell anything.

The third corollary of the Law of Risk is

Everything you do in a sales interview either raises or lowers the perception of risk and the fear of failure.

When you ask people to buy something, you are asking them to make a decision, to put their egos on the line. You are asking them to part with their money and gamble, to take a chance that you will deliver on your promises. For these reasons, and many more, the decision to buy is charged with emotion. Everything you do or say is important. It adds to or detracts from customers' perception of risk and uncertainty.

In any sales situation, and especially in a larger sale, nothing is neutral. Everything counts. Everything that you say either moves you toward the sale or moves you away from the sale.

Never allow yourself the luxury of saying, "That doesn't matter." Everything matters. *Everything counts.* Everything is either adding up or taking away. It's either helping or hurting. Your responsibility is to make sure that everything you do or say is helpful in some way in that it lowers the perception of risk and increases customers' feelings of security in buying from you.

How you can apply this law immediately:

1. Think of the likely risks that an intelligent customer might perceive in buying your product and getting the benefits that you promise in exchange for money. What could you do to reduce this perception of risk?

2. Ask your customers directly what risks they see in buying from you. What could you do to offset these specific risks and make your customers feel more comfortable making the buying decision?

66. The Law of Trust

—∞—

The trust bond between the salesperson and the customer is the foundation of the successful sale.

Trust is everything, especially in a large or complex sale. The higher the level of trust between you and your customer, the lower his or her fear of failure and perception of risk. When the level of trust is high enough, the sale will take place.

The first corollary of the Law of Trust is

You build a high-trust sales relationship by asking questions aimed at determining the real needs of the customer that your product or service can satisfy.

Most salespeople don't realize that a series of questions aimed at the customer's life and personal situation don't necessarily build the level of trust required to make a sale. These questions merely impress the customer with the idea that the salesperson is warm and friendly. They don't build credibility in the product or service.

It is only when you ask penetrating questions that identify needs that you can satisfy or uncover problems that you can solve that you are selling professionally. It is only when you ask good questions that help the customer understand his or her situation better that you are building trust and credibility.

The second corollary of the Law of Trust is

Successful salespeople listen twice as much as they talk.

Top salespeople practice the "70/30 Rule." They listen 70 percent or more of the time and they talk 30 percent or less of the time. It has often been said that you have two ears and one mouth, and in a sales conversation, you should use them in that proportion.

The best salespeople are superb listeners. They are quite comfortable asking questions and listening patiently to the answers. They are often low-keyed and friendly. Many of them are introverts and not particularly gregarious or outgoing. They are often quiet and reserved. They are also extremely effective.

The third corollary of the Law of Trust is

No one ever listened themselves out of a sale.

Many people talk themselves into and out of sales every single day, but it is hard to *listen* yourself out of a sale. In many cases, if you listen intently enough, if you listen patiently, and if you listen as though there were nothing else in the world more important than the words of the customer at that particular moment, you will listen yourself into more sales than you can imagine.

Very often, customers who start off uninterested in your offering will warm up to you and decide to buy from you for the simple reason that you listen well and you seem to care about them and their situation.

The fourth corollary of this law is
Listening builds trust.

There is no better and faster way to build trust between two people than for one to listen to the other. This is true in all relationships. You always like best the people who listen to you the most attentively when you want or need to talk about something that is important to you. Customers are the same. Customers think continually about themselves. They are preoccupied with their own concerns and problems. They always like and trust a person who listens carefully and intently when they talk about what is on their minds.

How you can apply this law immediately:

1. Structure your sales conversation around well-worded, well-thought-out questions that proceed from the general to the particular. Keep reminding yourself that "Telling is not selling."

2. Practice listening twice as much as you talk. Learn to be comfortable with silences in the sales conversation. The more you listen closely to your prospect, the better you will understand how to structure your offer so that it is exactly what he or she wants and needs.

67. The Law of Relationships

—⚬—

All selling is ultimately relationship selling.

People don't buy products or services. They "buy" the people who are selling the products or services. First, you sell yourself as a likable and credible person, and then you sell what you represent.

In its simplest terms, success in selling is determined by your ability to form high-quality relationships with your customers. Marketing and selling have changed dramatically in the last few years. Products and services are more complex and difficult to understand than ever before. Because of the higher levels of risk and uncertainty this creates, combined with the variety of options available to the customer, the relationship becomes central to selling anything.

The first corollary of this law is

The customer wants a relationship first.

To reduce risk and uncertainty, customers seek something that they can depend upon and believe in. And the one thing that we all have in common is that we all have relationships with other people, most of which are based on our intuition and our own good judgment.

Before customers will seriously consider a sales offer of any kind, they want to be sure that they can rely upon the salesperson and the company to fulfill their commitments after the money has changed hands. Customers today seek to build a relationship with the supplier before they move onto the decision of whether or not to buy.

Corollary number two of this law is

In complex sales, the relationship continues after
the sale.

Before customers buy a product or service, they are independent of the salesperson and the company. The customers don't need them in any way. However, once the customers have made the buying decision, they then become dependent upon the warranties and assurances given by the company for the satisfactory use and enjoyment of the product.

Because such a relationship continues after the sale, and often lasts as long as the customer uses the product or service, the decision to purchase a product or service is a decision to enter into a long-term relationship with the individual and the organization. If, for any reason, the customer is not comfortable with the idea of entering into this kind of long-term relationship, he or she will simply not buy the product or service in the first place.

The third corollary of the Law of Relationships in selling is

The relationship is more important than the
product or service.

Customers today, at least initially, view most products or services as *commodities* available from several sources. The customer who has decided to buy has to decide among competing suppliers, most of whom have similar prices and offer similar benefits. The customer almost invariably makes a choice on the basis of which salesperson and company the customer feels most comfortable entering into a business relationship with.

Because relationships are so important to customers, salespeople should tell their customers, in the course of sales conversations, that their philosophy and the philosophy of their company is to build long-term relationships with its customers. Tell your customers that you want to build and maintain a high-quality relationship throughout the period of time that they will be using the product or service.

The most successful salespeople and companies are those who establish long-term relationships with their customers. They make every effort to maintain the quality of those relationships through care, attentiveness, sensitivity, dependability, fast follow-up to complaints and requests, and excellent service and support.

Be sure to tell each customer that you want to build and maintain a long-term relationship with him or her. This is often the most important single factor in the buying decision.

How you can apply this law immediately:

1. Develop a process for relationship management. Maintain regular contact with your customers and your good prospects. Show them that you appreciate them by developing various ways to say "Thank you."

2. Spend fully 20 percent of your time and resources cultivating customers who have already bought from you. Beware of "relationship entropy," or taking customers for granted. This can be fatal to any sales relationship. Remember, the very best source of referrals is a happy, well-cared-for customer. Your job is to create and keep lots of them.

68. The Law of Friendship

—⚍—

A person will not buy from you until
convinced that you are a friend and acting in
his or her best interests.

This is called the "friendship factor" in sales. The undeniable fact is that almost all successful business relationships are built on friendships between the parties. Good salespeople are really excellent friend makers. They can easily turn strangers into friends wherever they go. They are relaxed, likable, and interested in other people. Other people like them, and in liking them, they want to do business with them.

We always prefer to conduct business with people we like. We are designed in such a way that we cannot and will not buy from people that we do not like, even if we want the product or service they offer.

The more business friendships you have, all things being equal, the more successful you will be and the more money you will earn in the field of selling.

How you can apply this law immediately:

1. To have a friend, you must first be a friend. Think of your prospects and customers as personal friends. How could you treat them so that they feel you really like and care for them?

2. Your best customers will tend to be the people you like the most and the people who most like you. What could you do to create and maintain more of these business friendships?

69. The Law of Positioning

—⁓—

The customer's perception of you and your company is his reality and determines his buying behavior with you.

The way your customer thinks about you, talks about you, and describes you to others determines everything he does or does not do in relation to you and what you sell.

Every product or service must be perceived positively by the customer before that customer can make any kind of buying decision. The most successful products and services are those that the customer perceives are from the most desirable and trustworthy suppliers of these products or services.

With proper positioning, your product or service will be seen by customers as the product of choice, against which others are compared. Some examples of excellent positioning are Coca-Cola, Kleenex, and Xerox. In each case, these products are the standard. When you refer to a drink, you say, "I feel like a Coke." If you have a runny nose, you ask someone to "get a Kleenex" for you. If you need a copy of a document, you ask someone to "make a Xerox of this." This dominant positioning gives these products an edge in the market, which translates into more and easier sales at higher prices with better profit margins.

The first corollary of the Law of Positioning is

Every visual element of dress, product, packaging, printing, and promotion creates a perception of some kind.

Nothing is neutral. Everything that you do or neglect to do, everything that the customer sees or fails to see, hears or does not hear, contributes to the customer's perception of you and your company. Everything counts.

The second corollary of the Law of Positioning is

Top salespeople position themselves as the preferred suppliers of their products and services.

Everything you do adds to the customer's perception of you as the ideal person to do business with when it comes to buying your particular product or service. The customer will often pay more for a similar product or service for no other reason than that it is *you* who is selling it and backing it up. Your position in the customer's mind can be so strong that no other competitor can get between you and the customer and replace you. The most successful companies and the most successful salespeople are those who have developed such strong positioning in their marketplaces that they are considered to be the standard against which competitors are compared.

How you can apply this law immediately:

1. Determine the *words* your customers use to describe you to others. How do they think about you, your products, your services, and your company overall? Do you know? Find out your exact positioning in your marketplace, and then decide what you could do to take maximum advantage of it.

2. Decide exactly how you want to be thought of by your customers. What are the exact words you would like them to use when they talk about you to others? What could you do, starting today, to build that perception in your customers' minds?

70. The Law of Perspective

—∾—

The way that you are viewed by your
customers determines your income.

Your reputation—how you are known to your customers, how
you are thought about and talked about by your customers when
you are not there—largely determines how much you sell and how
much you earn.

The first corollary of the Law of Perspective is

When you are viewed by your customer as working
for him or her, you will be in the top 10 percent of
money earners in your field.

Many thousands of customers have been interviewed exten-
sively about their buying habits and their reasons for selecting one
salesperson over another. The most common reason given is that
they feel that the salesperson really "works for me" rather than for
his or her own company. They feel that the salesperson cares more
about their needs than about making a sale or satisfying the
demands of the company that pays his or her wages.

When your customers begin talking about you and thinking
about you the same way that they talk and think about the very
best salespeople in your industry, you will start rising to that same
level yourself.

A very good question for you to ask yourself continually is,
How would it be useful for me to be viewed by my customers? If
you were a fly on the wall, and one of your customers was telling
one of your prospects about you, what would you want the customer to say?

Whatever it is, be sure that everything that you do in your interaction with each customer leaves him or her mentally prepared to say those things about you when you're not present.

The second corollary of the Law of Perspective is

Top money earners in sales are viewed as consultants, helpers, counselors, and advisors to their customers, not as salespeople.

Customers look upon top salespeople as friends who are trying to help them solve their problems or achieve their goals. They look upon those salespeople as partners and advisors. The customers do not perceive them as salespeople and they do not see themselves as being "sold" to. They see them more as teachers and helpers.

The more you try to help your customers get what they need and *teach* them how your products or services can help them, the more they will look upon you as a friend and the more they will buy from you. The more you behave in a way that creates the perception enjoyed by the top salespeople, the faster you will get the same results they do.

How you can apply this law immediately:

1. Determine how you want to be thought of by your customers. How would it be helpful for your customers to think about you and describe you? What can you do to create this perception in your customers' minds?

2. Position yourself as though you work for the customers rather than for your own company. Focus single-mindedly on the customers and their needs, their problems, their situations, and always talk in terms of how you can help them achieve their goals.

71. The Law of Advance Planning

—∿∿—

The best salespeople prepare thoroughly before every call.

This principle is so simple that it is often overlooked. The hallmark of the true professional is thorough preparation, reviewing every detail, before every sales meeting. The very best salespeople are those who review their presentations and study the details of their products and their sales materials repeatedly prior to every new sales contact.

You cannot imagine a top athlete who did not train regularly and warm up thoroughly before every competition. In fact, the period of training for an athlete consumes far, far more time than an actual competition itself. When you think of a crack military force, like the U.S. Marines or the Israeli Commandos, you think immediately of rigorous, disciplined training. In every field of endeavor, the most thoroughly trained and dedicated professionals rise to the top.

It is relatively easy to become a salesperson with little experience. But that is where the easy part ends. From then onward, hard, hard work and continuous training and preparation are essential for success. If you want to be the best and get the results that the best people get, you have to do the same things they do. And this means to prepare and prepare and then to *overprepare*.

The first corollary of the Law of Advance Planning is
The salesperson with the best knowledge of the customer's real situation will be the one most likely to make the sale.

The more time you take to thoroughly understand your prospective customer and your prospective customer's situation, the more likely you will be in a position to sell at the critical moment.

The second corollary of the Law of Advance Planning is

Sales professionals plan their questions in advance.

There is a direct relationship between the quality of the problem-focused questions that you ask a customer and the likelihood of a sale taking place. The only way of assuring that your questions are clear and penetrating is by writing them out, word for word, in advance. Some of the most successful salespeople who have ever lived have been "question experts."

Ben Feldman, a salesman for the New York Life Insurance Company, was written up in the *Guinness Book of Records* as the top salesman of all time. He was famous for spending two hours each night reviewing and rehearsing his material so that he would be sharp and well prepared the next day.

In his well-known book, *The Feldman Method,* Ben Feldman explains that his great success was largely due to his ability to ask the right questions at the right time. He discovered that a properly worded question could turn a neutral or negative prospect into an interested customer, sometimes in just a few seconds.

Heinz Goldman, in his book *How to Win Customers,* demonstrated that 95 percent of salespeople could improve their results by rewording their presentations. The choice of words in a question or a response can be very powerful, and the only way to be sure that you are using the best sentence construction is by writing, rehearsing, and practicing over and over.

The third corollary of the Law of Advance Planning is

The power is on the side of the salesperson with
the best notes.

Plan your sales-call objectives thoroughly in advance of meeting the client. Write down and itemize exactly what you hope to accomplish in this visit. After the call, quickly write down everything that was said. Don't trust it to memory. Remember the Chinese saying, "The palest ink lasts longer than the finest memory."

Prior to every sales call, and no matter how many times you may have visited this same customer, take a few minutes to review the customer's file, the customer's situation, and your own notes on what has taken place in the past. You'll be amazed at how impressive you sound when you go into a sales interview having just reviewed the customer's file a few minutes before. And customers always know if you have done your homework.

The top salespeople in every field prepare exhaustively prior to selling, prior to their presentations, and prior to closing. They think everything through in advance. And they leave nothing to chance. Remember, it's the details that make the difference. The salesperson who has taken the greatest amount of time to acquaint himself or herself with the most specific needs of the customer is the one who builds the highest level of trust and the best sales relationship. Thorough preparation is the essential precondition for successful selling.

How you can apply this law immediately:

1. Make it a habit to plan, prepare, and review thoroughly before every sales call. Create a checklist to go over before you leave your home or office. Resolve never to be caught not having done your homework in advance.

2. Keep excellent notes of every sales conversation. Write them up immediately after having met with the customer. Build a

customer file that could be passed on to another salesperson with no loss of momentum in the account. Never trust your memory.

72. The Law of Perverse Motivation

—∽∽—

Everyone likes to buy, but no one wants to be sold.

People don't like to feel that they are the recipients or the *victims* of a sales presentation. Most customers are independent in their thinking, and they don't like to think that they are being manipulated, pressured, or coerced into doing anything. They like to feel as though they are making up their own minds based on good information that has been presented to them.

The first corollary of the Law of Perverse Motivation is

The best salesperson is perceived as a helper who assists prospects in getting what they want and need.

Remember, it is the perception of the customers that, more than anything else, determines how the customers behave toward a salesperson. You must do everything possible to appear to be helping rather than selling.

The second corollary of the Law of Perverse Motivation is

Top salespeople are teachers who show their customers how products and services work to satisfy their needs.

The more you are perceived as a teacher, the more likely it is that you will also be perceived as a consultant and as an advisor.

You will be seen as a trusted counselor who can be depended upon to help customers get what they want by means of the product or service that you are selling.

If ever your customers feel, even for a moment, that you are trying to *sell* them into buying something, they will instantly resist and withdraw. The most important part of selling is the quality of the trust bond that exists between you and your customers. You can't afford to do anything that threatens that trust bond.

How you can apply this law immediately:

1. Think of yourself as a teacher and your sales presentation as a "lesson plan." Always begin your presentation by getting agreement on the value or benefit that the customer seeks that your product or service can deliver.

2. Design your presentation in such a way that you are always showing, explaining, and asking questions to assure agreement and understanding. See yourself as a teacher with a willing and able student, eager to learn.

Summary

All things are possible to the salespeople who *know* what they are doing, *believe* in what they are doing, and *love* what they are doing. If you are the right person selling the right product or service for the right company to the right customer, your future in sales can be unlimited.

To achieve your full potential in selling, to get into the top 10 percent of money earners in your field, you must follow the laws of selling. Your failure to know and obey any one of these laws can sabotage your efforts and decrease your sales. Everything counts!

CHAPTER SEVEN

The Laws of Negotiating

—∿—

The Laws of Negotiating

Your ability to get along with others is perhaps the most important skill you can develop if you really want to be successful and happy in business and in life. Today, everything involves relationships. The most successful people in almost every field are relationship experts. They have taken the time and made the effort to be very effective in their dealings with others, and this pays off for them in better jobs, higher pay, and more rapid promotion.

Perhaps the most valued form of intelligence in our society, the one that pays the most and the one that will make you the happiest, is "social intelligence." This is defined as the ability to interact and communicate effectively with others in a variety of situations.

Daniel Goleman of Harvard calls this quality "emotional intelligence," or "EQ." He shows that EQ is more important than IQ (intelligence quotient) in accounting for success in business and in life. The good news is that your emotional intelligence is not genetically determined or limited. It consists of a series of interpersonal skills you can learn via practice and repetition.

Your ability to interact with others to communicate, persuade, and negotiate determines your income more than any other factor. Your ability to get along well with others accounts for perhaps 85 percent of your happiness. It is therefore well worth your while to do everything possible to be very good in this area.

The Laws of Negotiating are closely related to economics. They are part and parcel of the same process. Both economics and negotiating are based on the fact that each person places different values on different things at different times. Everyone behaves *economically* in the sense that they always strive to negotiate the very best situation or result for themselves in each situation.

Every financial transaction or negotiation is based on the principle of *subjective value.* This principle states that a transaction is possible only when both parties value what they are getting *more* than they value what they are giving in trade. In a free society, commerce and trade take place only when both parties believe that, based on personal preferences, they will be better off exchanging with the other than they would be if they did not.

When you negotiate, you are always obeying the economic laws of *minimization* and *maximization.* You want to get the very most for the very least, all things considered. Whenever you are buying, selling, setting wages or salaries, either as an employer or an employee, or bargaining over the terms and conditions of a purchase or sale, you are negotiating in some way and trying to get the very best deal.

In a sense, all of life is a negotiation. When you are an infant, you negotiate for the attention of your parents by crying loudly to be fed or changed. Your currency in trade is hugs and kisses or just lying peacefully. Every child knows that expressions of happiness and affection can be traded for food, attention, warmth, toys, and other things, and children learn very early to trade this currency skillfully. Since it is all they have to trade, so to speak, they spend it carefully.

You are always negotiating in some way. When you drive from one place to another, you negotiate through traffic, getting in front of some people and letting others get in front of you. When you go to a restaurant, you negotiate, first of all, to get a table and then to get the kind of table you most like. You negotiate all the elements of your work life and everything you do or don't do. You negotiate prices, terms, schedules, standards, and a thousand other details all day long. The process is never ending.

In every relationship, a certain amount of negotiating and bargaining is going on continually. What you do and what the other person does in your marriage is continually being negotiated. You negotiate to get into the bathroom in the morning and to use the toaster at breakfast. You negotiate what you are going to do in your leisure time and where and how you are going to do it. You negotiate with your family, friends, and coworkers as naturally as breathing in and breathing out. It is not really a question of whether or not you negotiate. The only question is, How well do you do it?

One of your chief responsibilities in life is to learn how to negotiate well on your own behalf. You need to be able to get more of the things you want faster and easier than you could if the other person was better at negotiating than you.

The principle of *secondary consequences* applies to many negotiations as well. This principle says that often there are secondary consequences to be considered when you are negotiating, especially in a situation where you will need to interact with that person again sometime in the future. The very best negotiators are therefore those who can consider both the short term and the long term while negotiating. They seek satisfactory long-term outcomes in addition to getting the best deal at the moment.

Learning and practicing the Laws of Negotiating will help you to get more of the things you really want, better, faster, and easier than ever before. When you use these laws consistently, you will improve every aspect of your life.

73. The Universal Law of Negotiating

—m—

Everything is negotiable.

All prices and terms are set by someone. They can therefore be changed by someone. This does not mean that they will be changed, but it does mean that there is always a chance. When you begin looking at life as one long, extended negotiating process, you will find that almost every situation contains elements that you can negotiate to improve the terms and conditions for yourself and others.

The first corollary of this law is
Prices are a best-guess estimate of what the customer will pay.

This means that asking prices are only loosely connected to objective reality. The cost of manufacturing and marketing a particular product or service often has very little to do with the price that is put on it. Price is arbitrary and merely reflects someone's opinion of what the market will bear at that moment.

The second corollary of this law is
Every price was set by someone and can therefore be changed by someone.

Let me give you an example of this corollary. One day, I went into an expensive men's clothing store. It was in February, close to the end of winter. I saw a beautiful $500 cashmere overcoat that had been marked down to $350 and was prominently displayed on sale. I asked the salesclerk if he would sell that coat for $250.

The clerk was slightly shocked. He told me that that was impossible. No one ever negotiated prices in this kind of store.

What was written on the tag was the price of the coat and it couldn't be changed.

I realized immediately that I was dealing with a person who had no authority to negotiate. And the manager was out to lunch. So I very politely wrote down the amount, $250, on the back of my business card and told him to give it to his manager when he returned. I said that my offer would stay open until 3:00 P.M. that afternoon. Then I went back to my office.

At 2:30 P.M. the telephone rang and a very surprised salesclerk told me that he had gone to his manager, and his manager had agreed to accept the amount of $250 for the cashmere coat. Even the salesclerk was astonished because he had no idea that "everything is negotiable."

Don't be intimidated by written prices, either on signs or in letters or contracts. Assume that they are written in pencil and can easily be erased and replaced with something more favorable to you. The key is to ask.

How you can apply this law immediately:

1. Begin today to ask for better prices and terms, no matter what you are offered initially. The main reason that people don't ask for better terms and conditions is the deep subconscious fear of rejection that we all have. And the only way to overcome a fear is to confront it—to do the thing you fear until the fear goes away.

2. Make it a game to ask for better prices. Ask politely, ask in a warm and friendly way, ask positively, ask expectantly, and ask confidently. But be sure to ask. You will be amazed at how quick people are to improve the terms for you if you ask.

74. The Law of Futurity

—◌◌—

The purpose of a negotiation is to enter into an agreement such that both parties have their needs satisfied and are motivated to fulfill their agreements and enter into further negotiations with the same party in the future.

This is a foundation law of negotiating, and it applies especially to negotiations where you will be dealing with the same party again. In business, it is quite common for people to be in and out of business transactions and negotiations with each other for many years. This fundamental futurity must be kept in mind at each stage of each negotiation.

Let's break this law down into its constituent parts. First, "the purpose of a negotiation is to enter into an agreement." It is assumed, but not always true, that both parties want to do business together. If one does not and is merely negotiating for some other purpose, the other party can be at a considerable disadvantage.

The second part says, "such that both parties have their needs satisfied." This means that an agreement where one or the other party feels that he or she has *lost* does not fulfill the basic requirement of a successful negotiation. Both must feel that they have come out ahead.

This law then goes on to say, "and are motivated to fulfill their agreements and enter into further negotiations with the same party in the future." This means that both parties are satisfied enough with the outcome that they are motivated to fulfill whatever commitments they have made, and they feel positively enough about the deal that they are willing to negotiate again and enter into subsequent agreements in the future. Your job in every negotiation where you will be dealing with this person again is to assure that the other party will want to continue doing business with you in the future.

How you can apply this law immediately:

1. Analyze your current negotiating style. In what areas have you been more focused on "winning" in the short term without really considering the long-term damage that you might be doing to the relationship?

2. Look for ways to make the final agreement acceptable to the other party. Think of negotiating with this party again in the future based on the terms and conditions you are finalizing today. How could you improve the terms without sacrificing things that are important to you?

75. The Law of Win-Win or No Deal

—⁓—

In a successful negotiation, both parties should be fully satisfied with the result and feel that they have each "won" or no deal should be made at all.

Consistent with your determination to enter only into agreements that preserve long-term good relations between the parties, you should always seek an outcome that satisfies both. Remember, you always reap what you sow. Any settlement or agreement that leaves one party dissatisfied will come back to hurt you later, sometimes in ways that you cannot predict.

A very tough negotiator told me proudly about a hard deal he had wrung out of a national organization for the distribution of his company's products. He had demanded and threatened and negotiated an agreement that paid him considerably more, both in up-front payments and in percentages of sales, than any of the other clients for which this company distributed.

I happened to know the people on the other side quite well. I later asked them if the story was true. They confirmed that it was. I asked them how they would deal with their other clients when the terms became known, as they surely would. No problem, they told me. They had agreed to pay higher prices and royalties on everything they sold, but they had not agreed to sell any. And they didn't.

The businessman had negotiated a deal that was a "win-lose," with him winning and the others losing. But those on the losing side had no incentive to fulfill the implied commitment to market the products. They had no real incentive to go forward with this person, and no reason to ever want to do business with him again. To this day, they haven't.

In every ongoing negotiation, you should aim for a win-win solution, or no deal. When you enter into a negotiation where you will be dealing with this person again, you should be clear in advance that you are committed to reach a solution that is satisfactory to both. If it does not entail a win for both parties, you should simply refuse to make any deal at all.

When you are determined to achieve a win-win solution to a negotiation, and you are open, receptive, and flexible in your discussions, you will often discover a third alternative that neither party had considered initially but that is superior to what either of you might have thought of on your own.

For example, a husband and wife may want to take a summer vacation. He is adamant about going to the mountains and getting a chance to hike, and she is equally determined to go to the beach and sit in the sun. One or the other could win while the other loses.

Or, they could compromise and spend half of their vacation in the mountains and half of their vacation at the beach, leaving each of them dissatisfied for half the time. A third alternative, however, which could satisfy both of them, might be to go to a city like Vancouver, British Columbia, where the mountains meet the sea.

With this third alternative, during the day she could go to the beach and he could go to the mountains. They could both be together in the late afternoons, evenings, and early mornings and have a fully satisfying family vacation.

This kind of third alternative solution is almost always achievable if you are willing to look for it. It simply requires a commitment to win-win.

Once you've decided that you are only going to agree to a settlement that is satisfactory to both parties, this doesn't mean that you have to accept any arrangement that you consider second best. With your values and your intentions clear, you are now in a position to utilize every strategy and tactic available to you to get the very best deal for both of you—one that assures that you both end up happy with the arrangement.

How you can apply this law immediately:

1. Think win-win in all your interactions with others, at work and at home. Actively seek a middle way that satisfies the most pressing desires of both parties. Be creative in suggesting alternatives that get both you and the other person more of what you want.

2. Examine any situation you are in today that you are not happy with. How could you restructure the terms and conditions in such a way that the other person gets more of what he or she wants in the process of giving you more of what you want?

76. The Law of Unlimited Possibilities

—∞—

You can always get a better deal if you know how.

You never need to settle for less or feel dissatisfied with the result of any negotiation. There is almost always a way that you can get better terms or prices, whether you are buying or selling. Your job is to find that way.

The first corollary of this law is

If you want a better deal, ask for it.

The word "ask" is the most powerful word in the world of business and negotiating. Most people are so paralyzed by the fear of rejection and disapproval that they are afraid to ask for anything out of the ordinary. They just accept what is offered to them and hope for the best.

But this is not the case with the top negotiators. The top negotiators will quite calmly and confidently ask for any kind of price or term that is remotely within reason. You will be quite astonished at the better deals you will get by simply asking for a lower price if you're buying and asking for a higher price if you're selling.

One of my seminar graduates is a real estate salesman who buys houses. He works within a specific price range and looks at every home in that price range that comes on the market. His strategy is simple. Whatever the asking price, he offers 50 to 60 percent of that amount in cash, with no conditions. His offers all come with a short time limit.

He gets turned down dozens of times. Sellers often insult him and hang up on him. However, about one time in a hundred, he finds a "motivated seller," a seller who is eager to sell immediately, and the seller will accept his offer. He then arranges a first mortgage for an amount greater than he has agreed to pay and uses the mortgage money to buy the house. He then either rents the house for an amount in excess of the mortgage payment or resells it at a higher price. And his secret is simple. He just asks people to sell him their houses at far lower prices than anyone else would ever dare.

The second corollary of this law is

Whatever the suggested price, react with surprise and disappointment.

Remember, most people have plucked the price out of the air. They are always asking for more than they expect to get or offering less than they expect to pay. In either case, you should flinch and react with mild shock, no matter what the price or the offer. Appear hurt, as if the person has just said something cruel or unkind that was totally uncalled for. Then ask, "Is that the best you can do?" And remain perfectly silent.

Very often, when you ask a person how much an item is and you flinch when given the price, the person will lower the price immediately. Almost every price has a built-in cushion of available discount, and very often the salesperson will drop to that price with one painful flinch on your part.

The third corollary of this law is

Always imply that you can do better somewhere else.

There is nothing that causes a seller's price to drop faster than saying that you can get the same item cheaper from another source. This shakes the self-confidence of the salesperson, who immediately feels that he or she is going to lose the deal and often cuts the price quickly.

How you can apply this law immediately:

1. Negotiating is a skill that you can master with practice. Take every opportunity you can find to negotiate on smaller items, especially in situations where you don't really care about the outcome. Go to swap meets and garage sales and offer a fraction of the asking price. You will be amazed at how quickly you become skilled at getting better prices.

2. Do your homework. Check around and ask about other prices that are available. The more examples you can offer when you demand lower prices, the faster the other party will come down to a price that is acceptable to you.

77. The Law of Four

—⁓—

There are four main issues to be decided upon in any negotiation; everything else is dependent on these.

There may be dozens of details to be ironed out in a complex agreement, but the success or failure of the negotiation will turn on no more than four issues. I have spent two and three days in negotiating sessions with teams of skilled businesspeople on both sides of the table, discussing fifty pages of small and large details, only to have everything boil down to four key issues at the end.

The first corollary of the Law of Four is
Eighty percent or more of the content of the negotiation will revolve around these four issues.

This Law of Four and this factor of 80 percent turn out to be true in almost every case. No matter how long or complex the negotiation, no matter how many clauses, subclauses, and different details, or terms and conditions, at the end, you will find that most of the discussion, and the most important points of the negotiation, revolved around four basic items.

The second corollary of the Law of Four is

Of the four main issues in any negotiation, one will be the main issue and three will be secondary issues.

For example, you may decide to buy a new car. The four main issues to be decided might be price, trade-in value of your existing car, color, and accessories. Warranty and service policies will be important but secondary.

According to normal car-buying patterns, if you are going to buy a new car, you will probably consider about ten different cars and visit ten different dealerships. You will eventually settle on one model of car and approximately three dealerships that sell it. You will then make your decision based on the combination of these four elements, with price probably being the main issue and the other three varying in importance according to your individual situation and personal preferences.

The Law of Four can be extremely powerful if the two parties rank the importance of the four issues in different orders. One party may be more concerned about price and the other party may be more concerned about terms. This can lead to an excellent win-win solution that satisfies the most important needs of each party.

How you can apply this law immediately:

1. Think of something expensive and complex that you have purchased in the past. What were your four key considerations? What were the considerations of the other party? How did you finally reach an agreement?

2. Think of an upcoming negotiating situation in your work. Make a list of all your considerations and then order them by

importance to you. Make a list of the other party's considerations in order of importance. How can you use this information to get a better deal?

78. The Law of Timing

—⚭—

Timing is everything in a negotiation.

A negotiation can be made or unmade by the time at which it takes place. There is a "too soon" and a "too late" in every situation. Whenever possible, you must plan strategically and use the timing of the negotiation to your advantage. There is a better time to buy and a better time to sell in almost every case. And when your timing is right, you will always get a better deal than when it is not.

The first corollary of the Law of Timing is

The more urgent the need, the less effective the negotiator.

If you are in a hurry to close a deal, your ability to negotiate well on your own behalf diminishes dramatically. If the other person is eager to make the deal, he or she is functioning under a disadvantage that you can exploit to your advantage.

For example, every company has sales targets for each month, each quarter, and each year. Sales managers are tasked with hitting these numbers. They are dependent on them for their jobs, their incomes, and their bonuses. Every salesperson has a sales quota for each month as well. Therefore, when you are buying any large-ticket item, you will almost always get the best deal if you wait until the end of the month when the pressure is on to hit the targets.

The second corollary of the Law of Timing is
The person who allows himself or herself to be
rushed will get the worst of the bargain.

Rushing or using time pressure is a common tactic in negotiating, and you must be alert to other people trying to use it on you.
People will often tell you that you have to make up your mind
quickly or it will be too late. Whenever you hear this, you should
take a deep breath and patiently ask questions to find out just how
urgent the situation really is.

If someone insists that he or she needs an immediate decision,
you can reply by saying, "If you must have an answer now, then
the answer is no. But if I can take some time to think about it, the
answer may be different."

On the other hand, you can use this tactic to your advantage
by running out the clock so the other person has no time left and
has to make a decision on your terms. Just don't let someone else
do it to you.

The third corollary of the Law of Timing is
You resolve 80 percent of the vital issues of any
negotiation in the last 20 percent of the time
allocated for the negotiation.

Probably because of the prevalence of Parkinson's Law, which
says, "Work expands to fill the time allotted for it," most of the
key issues in a negotiation get jammed into the final phase of the
discussions. Up to this part of the negotiation, there seems to be a
natural human tendency to procrastinate on the resolution of the
most important issues.

What this means for you is that you must be patient in a negotiation. You must be prepared for the key issues to be resolved at
the last minute. Setting a schedule and a deadline for a decision

will help. If the key issues should happen to be resolved earlier, you can be pleasantly surprised. But this is the exception, not the rule.

A final point with regard to timing. Whenever possible, you should delay making an important decision. At the very least, don't allow the other person or persons to rush you into a decision by suggesting that if you don't act now, it will be too late. Whenever the item under negotiation involves a great deal of money, a long life of the product, or long duration of the decision, or it is the first time that you have negotiated in this area, buy time for yourself. Take at least twenty-four hours, if not an entire weekend, to think over your decision before acting. Use time as a weapon to strengthen your position and to improve your ability to make better decisions.

How you can apply this law immediately:

1. When you negotiate, set deadlines for the other party whenever possible. Remember the rule in sales, "No urgency, no sale!" You can always extend the deadline if the other party balks or disagrees.

2. Avoid deadlines for yourself whenever possible. Tell the other party that you are not going to make a decision today, no matter what is agreed to. Give yourself at least twenty-four hours to think it over before deciding. Sleep on it as a matter of course. You will be amazed at how much better you think when you have put some time between yourself and the decision.

79. The Law of Terms

—ന—

The terms of payment can be more important than the price in a negotiation.

Many products, such as homes and cars, are sold more on the terms of payment and the interest rates than on the actual price or even the product itself. People usually buy the most expensive home they can qualify for. People buy the most expensive car they can afford in terms of monthly payments. Your ability to vary the terms can be the key to success in a negotiation.

For example, I remember the first time I purchased a Mercedes-Benz. The salesman, a real professional, showed it to me and urged me to buy it. I loved the look of the car, but I told him that there was no way that I could afford it. It was too expensive and my income wouldn't allow it.

My mind-set was based on my previous experiences of buying cars, all of which had been financed over a three-year period. Over three years, the payments on the Mercedes would be out of my reach. The salesman then pointed out that, because it was a Mercedes and would hold its value, the car could be financed over five years rather than three. He then calculated what the monthly payments would be on a five-year amortization. In addition, by purchasing it through my business, I could deduct both interest payments and depreciation. As soon as I saw the actual number, I did a complete turnaround and agreed to buy the car, even though the price was far higher than I had envisioned paying.

The terms were more important than the price.

In another example, a friend of mine became extraordinarily successful as the general sales manager for a large home-construction company. His strategy was very clever. He realized that people did not buy homes, they bought down payments and monthly terms.

Instead of advertising the attractiveness of the homes and their sales prices, as his competitors were doing, he advertised the monthly payments required to purchase one of these new homes. His sales literally went through the roof, and he became one of the highest paid people in his profession.

The first corollary of the Law of Terms is
You can agree to almost any price if you can decide
the terms.

If you are negotiating and you really want to purchase the item, or sell it for that matter, and the price is the sticking point, shift the focus of your discussion and see if you can't negotiate *terms* that make it possible for the price to be more acceptable. Here's a true story that illustrates this strategy:

Two older businessmen owned land in the Tucson area, and one of them sold his land to a developer for a price of $1 million. A developer friend of mine wanted to purchase the land belonging to the second businessman, which was not as good a piece of land, but the second gentleman also wanted $1 million. As a matter of pride, he didn't feel that he could accept less than his friend had received for *his* land, even though the second man's property was not as attractive or as well located.

In negotiating the terms, however, it turned out that the seller didn't need the proceeds from the land. In fact, they would harm his tax position. He was actually planning to leave the land to his children and grandchildren.

So my developer friend agreed to pay $1 million for the land, but with no down payment, low annual payments, and a balloon payment at the end of twenty years. On that basis, the real, amortized cost of the land to the developer was considerably less, even though the sales price was listed at $1 million. The older businessman was satisfied and the sale went through very quickly.

The second corollary of the Law of Terms is

Never accept the first offer, no matter how good it sounds.

Even if the first offer is everything you could possibly ask for, don't accept it. Act a little disappointed. Ask for time to think it over. Ponder the offer carefully. Realize that no matter how good the first offer is, it usually means that you can get an even better deal if you are patient.

The third corollary of this law is

Never reject an offer out of hand, no matter how unacceptable it sounds when you first hear it.

A bad offer can be turned into a good deal for you if you can dictate the terms of payment. You can say, "That is an interesting suggestion. It is more (or less) than I had in mind. But let's see if there is a way that we can make it work."

How you can apply this law immediately:

1. Remember that you can get a better deal by controlling either the price or the terms. If the other party is determined to get the very best price possible, you can agree by suggesting terms that make the price acceptable.

2. Always look for ways to extend the actual payment of money as far into the future as possible. Any delay or deferment of payment, especially if you can arrange for no penalty for pre-payment, increases the attractiveness of the deal by lowering the cash outlay in the present.

80. The Law of Anticipation

—⁓—

Eighty percent or more of your success in any
negotiation will be determined by how well
you prepare in advance.

Action without planning is the cause of every failure.
Negotiating without preparation is the cause of just about every
poor deal that you ever get. The very best negotiators are those
who take the time to prepare the most thoroughly and to think
through the situation completely before negotiation begins.

The first corollary of this law is

Facts are everything.

The devil is in the details. The details are what trip you up
every single time. Be sure to get the facts before you begin negotiating, especially if the subject is large or complicated or both.
Don't be satisfied with the apparent facts or the supposed facts or
the obvious facts or the hoped-for facts or the assumed facts. Insist
on the real facts because the facts don't lie.

Avoid the temptation to accept superficial answers or incom-
plete numbers. Don't leap to conclusions. Avoid wishful thinking.
Do your research, ask questions, listen carefully, and take notes.
This can make an extraordinary difference to the outcome.

The second corollary of the Law of Anticipation is

Do your homework; one small detail can be all you
need to succeed in a negotiation.

In his best-selling book *My Life in Court,* the famous trial
lawyer Louis Nizer explained how, over a career spanning more
than 100 major trials, he was able to win life-and-death cases for
his clients because of the exhaustiveness of his preparation.

Sometimes, it was just one small fact that he had been able to uncover in many hours of research that made all the difference.

Corollary number three of the Law of Anticipation is

Check your assumptions; incorrect assumptions lie
at the root of most mistakes.

One of the assumptions that almost everyone makes when going into a negotiation is that the other party wants to make a deal in the first place. This may not be the case at all. You need to test this assumption.

Sometimes the other party has already decided to deal with someone else or not to buy or sell at all. Perhaps that party is just going through the motions of negotiating to see how good a deal he or she can get. Maybe someone else has offered to match the very best offer you can make. The other party may be negotiating without the authority or the ability to follow through on any deal you agree to. Be sure to check your assumptions before you invest too much time or emotion.

How you can apply this law immediately:

1. Think on paper. Write down every single detail of the upcoming negotiation. Note every term and condition you can think of. Then, identify your assumptions and begin gathering information to verify or reject them.

2. Whenever possible, talk to someone else who has negotiated the same sort of deal with the same person. Find out what the other person is likely to want and what he or she has agreed to in the past. Forewarned is forearmed!

81. The Law of Authority

—m—

You can negotiate successfully only with a
person who has the authority to approve the
terms and conditions you agree upon.

One of the most common of all negotiating ploys is called an
"agent without authority." This is a person who can negotiate with
you but who is not authorized to make the final deal. No matter what
is agreed upon, the agent without authority must check back with
someone else before he or she can confirm the terms of the agreement.

The first corollary of this law is

You must determine in advance if the other party
has the authority to make the deal.

The simplest way to do this is to ask the person if he or she is
authorized to act for the company or client. If it turns out that he
or she is not, you must be cautious about the positions you take
and the concessions you offer.

The Russians have been notorious for sending agents without
authority to international negotiating sessions over arms control,
trade, or foreign relations. The Americans would send negotiators
who were empowered to enter into agreements while the Russians
were empowered only to accept concessions. Who do you think
got the best and the worst of these sessions?

The second corollary of this law is

When dealing with someone who cannot make the
final decision, you must represent yourself as also
being unable to make the final decision.

Fight fire with fire. If the other person says that he or she cannot make the final decision, say that you are in the same position.

Anything you agree to will have to be ratified by someone else. This tactic levels the playing field and increases your flexibility in the case of an unacceptable counteroffer.

How you can apply this law immediately:

1. Make every effort to find out who makes the final decision before you begin negotiating. Ask the person you are talking to if he or she is empowered to enter into an agreement based on what you discuss. If not, find out who is and attempt to speak to him or her directly.

2. When you cannot deal with the final decision maker, do everything possible to find out exactly what he or she will find acceptable in making this decision. Be sure to mention that you will also have to get final approval before you can make an irrevocable decision to proceed. Keep your options open whenever possible.

82. The Law of Reversal

—⚭—

Putting yourself in the situation of the other person enables you to prepare and negotiate more effectively.

Before any negotiation that involves a good deal of money or a large number of details, use the "lawyer's method" of reverse preparation. This is a great technique that dramatically sharpens your negotiating skills.

In law school, student lawyers are often given a case to either prosecute or defend as an exercise. They are then taught to prepare the other lawyer's case before they begin preparing their own. They sit down and examine all the information and evidence, and they imagine that they are on the other side. They prepare that side thoroughly with the full intention of winning. Only when they feel that they have identified all the issues that the opposing lawyer will bring up do they then begin to prepare their side of the case.

You should do the same. Before you negotiate, write down everything that you think may be of concern to the person with whom you are going to be meeting. Writing things down clarifies them and enables you to see possibilities that you might otherwise have overlooked. When you have identified the major concessions that you think the other party will want, you can then think what you will offer in exchange. You can see where you are strong and where you are weak. You can identify possible areas where agreement or compromise is possible. This type of preparation by reversal is the hallmark of the superior negotiator.

A powerful tactic that you can use at the beginning of the negotiation is to open with this question: Why do you feel we are here, and what would you ideally like to accomplish in this discussion? This question will demonstrate to the other person that you are reasonable and open and interested in achieving a mutually satisfactory result. The other person will usually be quite willing to answer this question, and you will often be amazed at how quickly the two of you get down to substantive discussion.

How you can apply this law immediately:

1. Think through, discuss, and write out every concern or demand that you feel the other party might have *before* you meet with him or her to begin negotiating. Test these assumptions by asking the other party about his or her concerns and requirements.

2. Think of a current situation where you are not happy with an existing agreement. How could you examine this situation from the other person's viewpoint and make suggestions to

change the situation by offering something that he or she wants but is not currently getting?

83. The Law of Greater Power
—⚬—

The person with the greater power, real or imagined, will get the better deal in any negotiation.

Your ability to recognize both your power and the power of the other person is critical to your success in negotiating. Often you have more power than you know. Often the other party has less power than he or she appears to have. You must be clear about both.

The first corollary of the Law of Greater Power is
People will not negotiate with you unless they feel you have the power to help them or hurt them in some way.

In a negotiating session, you must have something the other person wants, or you must be able to withhold something he or she wants, for the other person to take you seriously. You must continually think about the situation from the other person's point of view so that you can position yourself for the maximum benefit to yourself.

The second corollary of this law is
Power is a matter of perception; it is in the eye of the beholder.

You can often create the perception of power, of being able to help or hinder a person in some way, with boldness and creativity.

Often when I am getting poor service on a flight or at a hotel, I will take out my pen and a piece of paper and politely but coldly ask the other person, "May I have your name, please?"

This invariably draws him or her up short. The person hesitatingly offers his or her name while mentally scrambling to figure out who I might be and why I might be asking. I then ask for the correct spelling. I carefully write the information down and put it away. From that moment on, the service improves dramatically. Whoever it is cannot take a chance that I might be a senior person in the company or someone who personally knows a senior person.

The three most important keys to negotiating are *power, preparation,* and *timing,* and of these three, power is often the most important and the most persuasive.

There are *ten* different types of power that you can develop and use, either individually or together, to influence and persuade the other party in any negotiation. The more important the issue to be negotiated, the more time you should take to consider how you can use one or more of these elements of power to strengthen yourself and your position.

The first is the power of *indifference.* The party who appears to be the most indifferent to whether or not the negotiation succeeds often has power over the other party if that other person wants the negotiation to succeed more than the first party. As a rule, you should always appear slightly detached and indifferent in a negotiation, as though you don't really care one way or the other.

The second form of power is the power of *scarcity.* Whenever you can suggest or imply that the item you are selling is in scarce supply and that others want it so the item will soon be sold anyway, you can influence the negotiation in your favor.

It is quite common in sales to suggest that a particular item has been so popular that it is almost out of stock, and the item that you are looking at is the last one that will be in stock for some time. Sometimes, people don't even realize how badly they want something until you suggest that they may not be able to get it at all.

The third form of power is that of *authority*. When you have an impressive title or you look as though you have the authority to make decisions, this image alone often intimidates the other person and enables you to get a better deal.

In his book *Winning through Intimidation*, author Robert Ringer writes about bringing two lawyers and a real estate agent with him to a meeting to discuss a real estate deal. The presence of three high-powered people at the negotiation enabled him to demand and get better prices and terms than he might have otherwise.

With regard to authority, a powerful image can really help you. Dress excellently, in every respect. Dress with power, in strong, conservative colors, looking like the president of a major corporation. When you look like a million dollars, the other party, especially if he or she is not as well dressed, will often be intimidated into giving you a better deal or will be much more responsive to your demands.

The fourth form of power is that of *courage*. You create the perception of courage by being willing to take risks, by speaking out clearly and forcefully and by being willing to either put yourself on the line for this deal or walk away from it. Whenever you act courageously by speaking up and demanding what you want, and offering to stand behind your demands, you demonstrate the kind of courage that gives you an image of power.

The fifth type of power is *commitment*. When you appear totally committed to making a negotiation a success, to finding a way to overcome any obstacle to agreement, you radiate an aura of power that often causes people to cooperate with you and go along with you.

The sixth form of power is that of *expertise*. The power of expertise comes from your making it clear that you are extremely well informed on the subject under negotiation. A person who is perceived as an expert in any situation has power over those who do not feel as knowledgeable. And the more research and preparation you have done in advance, the more knowledgeable you sound.

The seventh form of power you can create is called *knowledge of the needs of the other.* You develop this form of power by finding out everything you can about the other person before you begin negotiating. The more time you take to find out the exact situation of the other person, the more power you have in the negotiation.

Victor Kiam, the owner of Remington Corporation, tells about his negotiating for the purchase of a smaller company. The owner was asking a price of about $2 million. He had stated that the company was in extremely good shape and, therefore, worth every penny of it. Kiam found out who the bankers were for the company and then, by using his connections, found that the company was approaching insolvency and that the owner was desperate to sell.

Armed with this inside information, Kiam was able to negotiate a much better price in the eventual purchase of the company. Knowledge of the true needs of the other gave him a distinct advantage.

The eighth form of power you can develop is that of *empathy.* Human beings are predominantly emotional in everything that they do and say. When they feel that the person they are negotiating with empathizes with them and their situation, they are much more likely to be flexible and accommodating in the negotiation.

The picture of the tough-talking negotiator is largely fictitious. Every study of top negotiators shows that they are highly empathetic, low-keyed, solution oriented, and pleasant individuals to do business with. Good negotiators are usually very nice people. They make it clear from the beginning that they really care about finding a solution that everyone can live with.

The ninth form of power you can use is that of *rewarding or punishing*. When the other party perceives that you have the capacity to help or hurt him or her, the party is usually far more cooperative than if he or she doesn't feel you have this power.

The tenth and final form of power in negotiating is the power of *investment,* of either time or money or both. When you make it clear that you have invested a lot in the issue under negotiation, it gives you a form of power that you would not have if you had spent less time and effort.

For example, when I purchased my current house, I sat down with the owner and told him that my wife and I had looked at more than 150 houses and that this was the first house that we had decided to make an offer on. Even though the seller had had the house on the market for only a few weeks, he recognized immediately that we were serious and he negotiated with us in a serious way, leading to a satisfactory sale for him and a satisfactory purchase for us. If we had told him that this was one of the first houses we had looked at, his attitude might have been completely different.

In each case, your choice in negotiating is either to be influenced by or to have influence over the other party. The more of these elements of power that you can develop and use to your advantage in a negotiation, the more persuasive and effective you will be.

How you can apply this law immediately:

1. Prior to your next major purchase, sale, or negotiation of any kind, review the different forms of power described here and think about how you can use them to give yourself an advan-

tage. Write out and discuss your thinking with someone else to be sure that you are completely prepared.

2. Practice the power of indifference in every negotiation as a matter of course. When you appear unconcerned or uninterested in the success of the negotiation, you will often unnerve the other party and induce concessions from him or her before you have even taken a position or made an offer.

84. The Law of Desire

The person who most wants the negotiation
to succeed has the least bargaining power.

The more you want to make the purchase or sale, the less power you have. Skilled negotiators develop the art of appearing polite but uninterested, as if they have many other options, all of which are as attractive as the situation under discussion.

The first corollary of the Law of Desire is
No matter how badly you want something, you
should appear neutral and detached.

The more important something is to you, the more important it is for you to appear unemotional, unaffected, and unreadable. Don't smile or appear interested in any way. An attitude of mild boredom is best.

The second corollary of the Law of Desire is
The more you can make the other party want it,
the better deal you can get.

This of course, is the essence of successful selling. Focus all your efforts on building value and pointing out the benefits the other party will enjoy when he or she makes the purchase or sale. Desire is the critical element.

Chinese jade dealers were famous for showing one item of jade at a time to a prospective customer. The Chinese, by long custom, would keep their faces completely unemotional and inscrutable. However, when the dealer revealed a piece of jade that the customer really liked, the pupils of the customer's eyes would dilate widely. The jade dealer would be watching carefully for this and when he saw the pupils dilate, he knew which item the customer wanted the most and which one he could negotiate on the most effectively.

How you can apply this law immediately:

1. Before you begin negotiating, make a list of all the benefits of dealing with you. Organize the list by priority, from the most persuasive benefit through to the least persuasive. Mention these key benefits in the course of the negotiation and be alert to the other party's reaction.

2. Always be polite and friendly during the negotiation. This makes it easier for you to change your mind, to make concessions, and to compromise without your ego getting in the way. It also makes it easier for the other party to make concessions and agree at the appropriate time.

85. The Law of Reciprocity

—⁓—

People have a deep subconscious need to reciprocate for anything that is done to or for them.

The Law of Reciprocity is one of the most powerful of all determinants of human behavior. This is because nobody likes to feel that he or she is obligated to someone else. When someone does something nice for us, we want to repay that person, to reciprocate. We want to be even. Because of this, we seek an opportunity to do something nice in return. This law is the basis of the law of contract, as well as the glue that holds most human relationships together.

This Law of Reciprocity is applied most actively in negotiating when the issue of concessions comes up. Ideally, every concession in a negotiation should be matched by a concession of some kind on the part of the other person. The giving and getting of concessions is often the very essence of a negotiation.

The first corollary of the Law of Reciprocity is
The first party to make a concession is the party
who wants the deal the most.

You must therefore avoid being the first one to make a concession, even a small concession. Instead, be friendly and interested, but remain silent. The first person to make a concession will usually be the person who makes additional concessions, even without reciprocal concessions. Most purchasers and sellers are aware of this. They recognize that early concessions are a sign of eagerness and are prepared to take advantage of it. Be careful.

The second corollary of the Law of Reciprocity is
Every concession you make in a negotiation should
be matched by an equal or greater concession from
the other party.

If the other party asks for a concession, you may give it, but never without asking for something else in return. If you don't request a reciprocal concession, the concession that you give will be considered to have no value and will not help you as the negotiation proceeds.

If a person asks for a better price, suggest that it might be possible but you will have to either decrease the quantity or lengthen the delivery dates. Even if the concession is of no cost or value to you, you must make it appear valuable and important to the other party or it will not help you in the negotiation.

The third corollary of the Law of Reciprocity is
Small concessions on small issues enable you to ask for large concessions on large issues.

One of the very best negotiating strategies is to be willing to give something in order to get something. When you make every effort to appear reasonable by conceding on issues that are unimportant to you, you put yourself in an excellent position to request an equal or greater concession later.

How you can apply this law immediately:

1. Use the reciprocity principle to your advantage. Before negotiating, make a list of the things the other party might want and decide upon what concessions you are willing to give to get what you want. This preparation strengthens your negotiating ability considerably.

2. Prepare your best price or offer before you begin. Then, think through your first "fallback" position and how far you are willing to go to make a deal. Prepare your final fallback position as well, along with the maximum you are willing to concede. This exercise of thinking through these issues in advance will make you a much better negotiator.

86. The Walk Away Law

—⁓—

You never know the final price and terms until you get up and walk away.

You may negotiate back and forth, haggling over the various details of the deal for a long time, but you never really know the best deal you can get until you make it clear that you are prepared to walk out of the negotiation completely.

When I was living in Mexico, I would often barter and buy things in the markets and bazaars. I found that you could go back and forth for a long time but that you never really knew how far down in price the seller would go until you shrugged your shoulders, thanked him for his or her time, and walked away. Once I had to walk an entire city block, without turning and looking back, before the owner of the store broke and came running after me and sold me the item at the final price that I had offered.

The first corollary of the Walk Away Law is

The power is on the side of the person who can walk away without flinching.

When you do walk out, always be pleasant, low-keyed, and polite. Thank the other person for his or her time and consideration. Leave the door open so that you can enter back into the negotiation with no loss of face.

The second corollary of this law is

Walking out of a negotiation is just another way of negotiating.

Some of the very best negotiators, both nationally and internationally, are extremely adept at getting up and walking out. They will leave the room, the building, the city, and even the country, if necessary, to strengthen their positions and increase their perceived power in a negotiation.

A common tactic, when teams are negotiating, is for one or more of the key players on one team to get up angrily, storm out of the room, and vow never to come back. However, they will leave behind someone who will then seek some way to make peace with his or her partners and bring them back into the discussion. The remaining party will be friendly and accommodating, as if really on the side of the other people. This tactic is very common in labor-management negotiations.

Another version of this is called "good guy–bad guy." In this version, there will be two negotiators, or interrogators in police investigations, one of whom will be hard and demanding while the other will be friendly and accommodating. One will be unreasonable while the "good guy" will try to make peace by getting you to concede a little to placate the "bad guy." It is all part of the game, and you need to be aware of it in case anyone ever tries to use it on you.

How you can apply this law immediately:

1. Be prepared to get up and walk out of a negotiation before you go in. Make sure everybody on your team knows about this and when to do it. At the appropriate moment, you all stand up and head for the door. This will often completely confuse and disorient the other party or parties.

2. Be prepared to cut off a negotiation the very minute you get an unacceptable offer or condition. Close up your briefcase, thank the other person for his or her time, and head for the door. The better you get at this, the better deals you will get.

87. The Law of Finality

—⚬⚬⚬—

No negotiation is ever final.

It often happens that once a negotiation is complete, one or both parties thinks of something or becomes aware of an issue that has not been satisfactorily resolved. Maybe circumstances change between the signing of the agreement and its implementation. In any case, one of the parties is not happy with the result of the negotiation. One party feels that he or she has "lost." This is not acceptable if the two parties are anticipating negotiating and entering into further deals in the future.

The first corollary of the Law of Finality is

If you are not happy with the existing agreement,
ask to reopen the negotiation.

Most people are reasonable. Most people want you to be happy with the terms agreed upon in a negotiation, especially if the terms are carried out over a long period of time. If you find that you are not happy with a particular term or condition, don't be reluctant to go back to the other person and ask for something different.

Think of reasons why it would be beneficial to the other person to make these changes. Don't be afraid to point out that you are not happy with this situation and you would like to change the agreement so that it is more fair and equitable to you.

The second corollary of the Law of Finality is

Use zero-based thinking on a regular basis by asking
yourself, If I could negotiate this arrangement over
again, would I agree to the same terms?

Be willing to examine your previous decisions objectively by applying zero-based thinking. Be prepared to ask yourself, If I had not made this agreement, knowing what I now know, would I enter into it? This ability to continually reevaluate your previous decisions, to get your ego out of the way, and to look honestly and realistically at your ongoing situation is the mark of the superior negotiator.

How you can apply this law immediately:

1. Review your current situation and especially those ongoing arrangements with which you are dissatisfied in any way. Think about how you could reopen the negotiation and what sorts of terms and conditions would be more satisfactory to you.

2. Whenever you experience stress or unhappiness with the existing agreement, or whenever you feel that the other party is dissatisfied, take the initiative to revisit the agreement and find a way to make it more satisfying for both parties. Think long term.

Summary

Negotiating is a normal and natural part of life. You owe it to yourself to become very skilled at it. As in anything else, the key to excellence is for you to practice at every opportunity. Make it a game.

Ask for what you really want. Ask for better prices, better terms, better conditions, better interest rates—better everything. Realize that you can save yourself the equivalent of months and even years of hard work by learning how to become an excellent negotiator on your own behalf. And you can if you think you can. You can if you just *ask*.

CHAPTER EIGHT

The Laws of Time Management

—∞—

88. The Law of Clarity

89. The Law of Priorities

90. The Law of Posteriorities

91. The Law of the Most Valuable Asset

92. The Law of Planning

93. The Law of Rewards

94. The Law of Sequentiality

95. The Law of Leverage

96. The Law of Timeliness

97. The Law of Practice

98. The Law of Time Pressure

99. The Law of Single Handling

100. The Law of Competence

The Laws of Time Management

—◇—

Everything you are today and everything you become in the future will be determined by the way you think and the way you use your time. Your attitude toward time is a critical factor in all you do and everything you accomplish.

When I began to study successful people, I found that they all had a common characteristic. They were all described as being "extremely well organized."

Successful people have developed the ability to get a lot more done in the same period of time as unsuccessful people. They have clear goals and objectives, clear and specific plans, and well-organized calendars that enable them to focus continually on the most valuable uses of their time.

My greatest paradigm shift regarding time came when I revised my thinking about my personal relationship to time management some years ago. Up to that point, I had seen myself as the "sun" of my universe, with all of the planets, or factors of my life, orbiting around me in great circles, sometimes coming closer and at other times moving away.

One of these planets was "time management," which went into and out of orbit as I came across a book, an article, or a tape on time management techniques.

The big change for me came when I reversed this view and I realized that time management was actually the sun of my life and all of the factors of my life were the planets that orbited around that. I suddenly realized that by getting complete control of my time, every other part of my life would fall into place as well. And so they did.

Very often, people of equal abilities and similar backgrounds enter into a competitive field at the same level of responsibility and income. Ten years later, however, some of these people are earning five times and ten times as much as the others who started with them at the same time. These top people have corner offices and greater responsibilities. They are highly respected and esteemed by their coworkers and colleagues. They have better lives, nicer homes, and happier families.

And the one thing they all have in common is that they seem to get far more done in the same amount of time as the people around them. They use the minutes and hours of each day differently. They are far more productive. And as they get more done, they are given more and more to do and more things of greater value. They are then paid more and promoted faster.

The good news is that when you learn and practice the same time management techniques, these universal laws and principles of time usage, you immediately begin moving onto the fast track in your own life. You put your foot on the accelerator of your own career. You begin to accomplish more things faster in your work and personal life than ever before.

People who practice these laws of time management report that their careers take off, their incomes increase, and surprisingly enough, they have much more time to spend with their families and friends.

The Laws of Time Management are timeless and eternal. They work everywhere and for everyone. When you align your activities in harmony with these laws and principles, you will begin to accomplish vastly more than you ever thought possible.

88. The Law of Clarity

—m—

The clearer you are about your goals and
objectives, the more efficient and effective
you will be in achieving them.

Clarity accounts for probably 80 percent of success and happiness. Lack of clarity is probably more responsible for frustration
and underachievement than any other single factor. That's why we
say that "Success is goals, and all else is commentary." People with
clear, written goals accomplish far more in a shorter period of time
than people without them could ever imagine. This is true everywhere and under all circumstances.

You could even say that the three keys to high achievement are
"Clarity, Clarity, Clarity," with regard to your goals. Your success
in life will be largely determined by how clear you are about what
it is you really, really want.

The more you write and rewrite your goals and the more you
think about them, the clearer you will become about them. The
clearer you are about what you want, the more likely you are to do
more and more of the things that are consistent with achieving
them. Meanwhile, you will do fewer and fewer of the things that
don't help to get the things you really want.

Here, once more, is the simple, seven-step process that you can
use to achieve your goals faster and easier than ever before.

First, decide exactly what you want in each area of your life.
Be specific!

Second, write it down, clearly and in detail.

Third, set a specific deadline. If it is a large goal, break it down
into subdeadlines and write them down in order.

Fourth, make a list of everything you can think of that you are going to have to do to achieve your goal. As you think of new items, add them to your list.

Fifth, organize the items on your list into a plan by placing them in the proper sequence and priority.

Sixth, take action immediately on the most important thing you can do in your plan. This is very important!

Seventh, do something every day that moves you toward the attainment of one or more of your important goals. Maintain the momentum!

Fewer than 3 percent of adults have written goals and plans that they work on every single day. When you sit down and write out your goals, you move yourself into the top 3 percent of people in our society. And you will soon start to get the same results that they do.

Study and review your goals every day to be sure they are still your most important goals. You will find yourself adding goals to your list as time passes. You will also find yourself deleting goals that are no longer as important as you once thought.

Whatever your goals are, plan them out thoroughly, on paper, and work on them every single day. This is the key to peak performance and maximum achievement.

How you can apply this law immediately:

1. Make a list of ten goals that you would like to achieve in the coming year. Write them down in the present tense, as though a year has passed and you have already accomplished them.

2. From your list of ten goals, ask yourself, What one goal, if I were to accomplish it, would have the greatest positive impact on my life? Whatever it is, put a circle around this goal and move it to a separate sheet of paper.

3. Now, practice the seven-step method described above on this goal. Set a deadline, make a plan, put it into action, and work

on it every day. Make this goal your major definite purpose for the weeks and months ahead.

Get ready for some amazing changes in your life.

89. The Law of Priorities

—∙∞∙—

Your ability to set clear and accurate priorities on your time determines the entire quality of your life.

The very worst use of your time is to do very well what need not be done at all. The Pareto Principle says that 20 percent of your activities will account for 80 percent of the value of your activities. This means that if you have a list of ten items to accomplish, two of those items will be worth more than the other eight items altogether.

To achieve great things, you must always be concentrating on the small number of activities that contribute the greatest value to your life and your work.

The value of anything in your order of priorities can be measured by assessing the potential *consequences* of doing it or not doing it. Something that is important has significant consequences to your life and your career. Something that is unimportant has few or no consequences of significance to your life or career. The mark of the superior thinker is the ability to consider possible consequences before taking action.

Continually ask yourself, What is the most valuable use of my time, right now? And whatever it is, work on *that*.

Your ability to discipline yourself to work on those few tasks that can make the greatest difference in your life is the key quality that makes everything else possible for you.

How you can apply this law immediately:

1. Make a list of everything that you do as part of your job. Now, analyze the list and select the three to five things that are more important than everything else put together.

2. Imagine that you are going to receive a $100,000 bonus at the end of the month if you can work on your highest priority items every minute of every day. How would that change your behavior? What would you do differently?

90. The Law of Posteriorities

—◆—

Before you start something new, you must discontinue something old.

You can gain control of your life only to the degree to which you stop doing things that are no longer as valuable or as important to you as other things you could be doing.

You already have too much to do and too little time in which to do it. The average person today is working at about 110 percent of capacity or more. Your dance card is full. You do not have any spare time.

As your life changes, your priorities change as well. Certain things that were important at one stage of your life or career are no longer as important as you move to another stage of your life or to another level of responsibility.

You must continually ask yourself, What activities in my life can I cut back on, delegate, or discontinue to free up more time for my most important activities?

To start anything new, you must stop doing something old. We say that "getting in means getting out." Analyze your time carefully and have the courage to stop doing things that are no longer as important to you as other things could be.

Starting up means stopping off. Getting in requires getting out. You cannot take on something new without deliberately deciding to discontinue something else. What is it going to be?

How you can apply this law immediately:

1. Analyze your work and make a list of the items that consume most of your time. Which of these activities could you discontinue or delegate to free up more time for higher value work?

2. Compare your daily activities against your annual income. Would you pay someone else your equivalent salary to do the things that you are doing? If you wouldn't, stop doing those things immediately and pass them on to someone who can do them almost as well as you can.

91. The Law of the Most Valuable Asset

—m—

Your most valuable asset is your earning ability.

An asset is something that yields a steady, predictable cash flow. Your ability to earn money is probably the most valuable asset you have.

Your ability to work, to produce, to earn money in our competitive economy by applying your brain and ability to your world enables you to generate tens of thousands of dollars each year. You could lose everything, all your possessions, but as long as you maintain your earning ability at a high level, you can continue to enjoy one of the highest standards of living in the world.

It has taken you your entire lifetime to develop your earning ability to where it is today. But your earning ability is a *depreciating* asset, like a car or a piece of equipment. You must continually maintain and upgrade the quality of your earning ability to keep yourself at the same high level of productivity, performance, and output.

Knowledge and skill are the keys to the twenty-first century. Your earning ability is made up of your unique combination of knowledge and skills developed to their current levels. If your industry is undergoing rapid *change*, your knowledge and skills are also undergoing rapid *obsolescence*. You must continually replace old knowledge and skill with new knowledge and skill if you want to keep even, much less get ahead.

You are being paid today exactly what you are worth, no more and no less, based on your current earning ability. If you want to increase your standard of living, you must increase your earning ability through a systematic and deliberate process of learning and practicing new skills and abilities.

How you can apply this law immediately:

1. Identify the specific skills you have that make you the most valuable to your organization. Which are essential to generating your income? Whatever your answers, make a plan to improve in each of these critical skill areas.

2. Look down the road of your life. What will you absolutely, positively have to be excellent at doing three to five years from now for you to continue enjoying your current or an even higher standard of living? Whatever it is, identify these core competencies and then make a plan to acquire them.

92. The Law of Planning

—∿—

Every minute spent in planning saves ten minutes in execution.

The purpose of strategic planning in a corporation is to reorganize and restructure the activities and resources of the company so as to increase the "return on equity," or return on the money invested and working in the company. The purpose of "personal strategic planning" is for you to increase your "return on energy," the return on the mental, emotional, physical, and spiritual capital you have invested in your life and career.

Every minute that you spend planning your goals, your activities, and your time in advance saves ten minutes of work in the execution of those plans. Therefore, careful advance planning gives you a return of ten times, or 1,000 percent, on your investment of mental, emotional, and physical energy.

It takes only about 10–12 minutes for you to make up a plan for your day. This investment of 10–12 minutes will save you 100–120 minutes in execution. This is an increase in productive time of approximately two hours per day, or a 25 percent increase in productivity and performance, in ROE, from the first day that you begin planning your day in advance.

The key to personal efficiency is for you to use a good time planner. Virtually any planner will work if you will discipline yourself to use it as the core of your time management system. Today, Palm Pilots and personal digital assistants (PDA), in combination with personal computers, can enable you to plan your time with greater efficiency than has ever been possible.

Begin with a master list as the foundation of your time planning system. Write down everything that you can think of that you will need to do for the indefinite future. As new ideas, goals, tasks, and responsibilities arise, write them down on your master list. Don't trust them to memory.

Plan each month in advance by transferring the appropriate items from your master list to your monthly list. This is best done the last week of each month.

Plan each week in advance by transferring items from your monthly list to your weekly list. This is best done the weekend before.

Plan each day in advance by transferring items from your weekly list to your daily list and by then adding anything else that needs to be done that day. This is best done the night before.

Plan every project, meeting, and goal in detail, before you begin. The very act of planning forces you to think better and more accurately about everything you do. The more you think about and plan something, on paper, the faster and more efficiently you will accomplish it when you start work.

Regular planning assures that you spend more time on activities of higher value. This increases your effectiveness and your efficiency in everything you do. Perhaps the most important rule of all is for you to "Think on paper!"

Work from a list. Always write down your tasks and activities before you begin. Use this list as your blueprint.

How you can apply this law immediately:

1. Impose a sense of order on your life by making a detailed list of every single thing you have to do for the foreseeable future.

2. Analyze your list carefully and set clear priorities on the items before you begin. Never give in to the temptation to clear up small things first.

3. Discipline yourself to work only on those activities that have the most significant impact and influence on your life. Get them done quickly and well. Once you develop this habit of

planning and prioritizing, your stress level will decline, your productivity will increase, and your career will take off.

93. The Law of Rewards

—⚋—

Your rewards will always be determined by your results.

You will always be paid in direct proportion to what you do, how well you do it, and the difficulty of replacing you. We live in a meritocracy where we are always rewarded in direct proportion to the results we get for others.

The fastest way for you to get paid more and promoted faster is for you to achieve a greater quality and quantity of results for your company and for yourself. People who enjoy high incomes and high standards of living are people who are getting more and better results than others in whatever it is that they are doing.

Focus on accomplishments rather than activities. Continually look for ways to get more and better results, faster than before. Regularly assess each of your activities and make sure that what you are doing is contributing the greatest possible quantity and quality of results at any given time.

Keep asking yourself, What outcomes are expected of me? Always look for ways to do more than you are paid for. Go the extra mile. There are never any traffic jams on the extra mile.

How you can apply this law immediately:

1. Continually ask yourself, Why am I on the payroll? What specific *results* have you been hired to accomplish? What results, if you failed to get them, would jeopardize your job and your career?

2. Identify the most important things you do each day. How could you get better in each area? What could you do to make yourself indispensable?

3. Go the extra mile. In what ways could you do *more* than you are paid for? When you consistently do more than you are paid for, you will eventually be paid far more than you are receiving today.

94. The Law of Sequentiality

—〰—

Time management enables you to control the sequence of events in your life.

A positive mental attitude, an attitude of optimism and confidence, increases your energy, your creativity, and your capacity to get greater results. And a positive mental attitude is rooted in your feeling that you have a "sense of control" over your life. This sense of control is the key issue in peak performance.

When you have too much to do and too little time, you can start to feel overwhelmed. You begin feeling that you are losing control of your time. Time management, however, is the tool that you can use to control the sequence of events and thereby take complete control of your life.

You are always free to choose what you do *first,* what you do *second,* and what you do *not at all.* Your entire life today is the sum total result of the quality of your choices and decisions to this moment. If you are not happy with any part of your life, it is up to you to begin to make different choices and better decisions.

The starting point of making better decisions is for you to stop making worse decisions. At any given moment, you can stop the clock and decide to change the sequence of events in your life.

By changing the sequence of events, by deciding to do things in a different order, you can change your entire life and all of your results.

You take complete control of your life and your future by taking control of the sequence of events, by deciding to do certain things *before* you do other things. By making new choices and better decisions, you put your hands on the wheel of your own life and steer it in the direction that you really want to go.

How you can apply this law immediately:

1. Analyze the way you spend a typical day or a typical week. What are the things that you need to do more of, sooner, in order to improve the quality and quantity of your output and results?

2. Identify the choices and decisions that you have made in the past that have created the problems and difficulties you are wrestling with today. Whatever they are, begin immediately to make new choices and decisions that will take you in a new direction in your life.

3. Take control of the *sequence of events* in your life. Take complete control of your future. What changes can you make immediately to improve the overall quality of your life and work? Whatever they are, resolve to make them today.

95. The Law of Leverage

—⌇—

Certain things you do enable you to
accomplish vastly more than you would if
you spent the same amount of time in other
activities.

Your goal should be to become a *multiplication sign* in your
own life. By selecting the one or two things that you can do that
can make an extraordinary difference in your results, you can dramatically increase your value to your company and to yourself.

One multiplication factor that you can find and use is a "*point
of intensity.*" A point of intensity is something that can have
tremendous impact on the activities of other people. For example,
a decision to embark on a particular course of action, to make an
investment, to get in or to get out of some activity, can affect the
activities of many other people and, through them, the entire
future of a business. What are your potential "points of intensity"?

Archimedes, the Greek philosopher, once said, "Give me a
lever long enough and a place to stand and I can move the world."
What are the activities you engage in that have tremendous leverage in that they affect the activities of other people and the use of
other resources?

Some of the most common forms of leverage in business are
"other people's money," "other people's knowledge," and "other
people's efforts." We refer to them as OPM, OPK, and OPE.

Other people's money is money that you can borrow to leverage your business activities, to buy and sell greater amounts than
would be possible if your activities were limited to your own financial resources. This is the major reason for using credit in business
and investments. Your ability to gain access to other people's
money for these purposes can be a critical factor in your success.

Other people's knowledge is another leverage factor. Your ability to tap into the knowledge and experience of others, to get the key information and ideas you need to get ahead, can enable you to leverage your resources and get far greater results than someone who tries to get results on his or her own.

Other people's efforts refers to the time and energy you can acquire by hiring other people who have the key skills and abilities that you need to maximize or leverage your own talents and resources.

By developing your ability to pull together other people's efforts, other people's knowledge, and other people's money, you can accomplish vastly more in the same period of time than someone who is forced to rely on his or her own personal energy and resources.

How you can apply this law immediately:

1. Determine the one or two things that you can do that, if done well and in a timely fashion, could result in the greatest payoff for you and your organization. How could you reorganize your time to focus exclusively on these critical areas?

2. Develop a plan to acquire and employ other people's knowledge, efforts, and money. What could you offer to attract the support you need so you can move ahead faster in your business and your career?

96. The Law of Timeliness

—⟪⟫—

The ability to act faster than anyone else can
be your greatest asset.

Time is the currency of the twenty-first century. Your ability to set priorities and then to move fast and get the job done quickly and well is the most valued set of time management skills in the workplace today.

Develop a "sense of urgency." Only 2 percent of the population have a sense of urgency, and they eventually outpace everyone else.

People today are impatient. Even instant gratification is no longer fast enough. Speed and execution are associated with value in people's minds. When you get a reputation for being the kind of person who gets the job done fast, responsibilities, opportunities, and rewards will gravitate toward you like iron filings to a magnet.

When you want to get something done, give it to a busy person. Busy people work at a faster tempo than average people do. They get a lot more done in the same period of time. Your job is to develop a reputation for being the fastest moving person in your workplace. Start a little earlier, work a little harder, and stay a little later.

Work in "real time"—move quickly on small urgent tasks. Get them done and out of the way immediately. Pick up the pace. Move faster, get it done now. Don't waste time. Sometimes, your ability to take the job and get it done faster than anyone else is all you need to be a great success.

How you can apply this law immediately:

1. Always be looking for ways to get the job done faster. What are your key outputs and how could you complete them more quickly than ever before?

2. Reorganize your work so that you can give your boss and your customers what they need, faster. One good idea to cut the length of time it takes to complete a task can give you an edge in the marketplace.

3. Look for ways to serve your customers faster than your competitors. Every breakthrough in business and technology today

involves serving customers faster than someone else. Do it. Fix it. Try it. Move fast. Someone is gaining on you!

97. The Law of Practice

—w—

Continuous practice of a key skill reduces
the time required to perform the task and
increases the output achieved.

The more you practice a key skill, the less time it takes you to perform the same task. The better you get at a particular job, the more of that job you can do in a shorter period of time. The greater the skill you develop in your work, the higher the quality of the work you can do and the less time it takes you to do it.

A highly skilled typist can type five to ten times as much as an unskilled typist and do better work. The two typists may have the same age, intelligence, and natural abilities, but the faster typist has developed the skill that enables her to outproduce the other by several times.

Use the "learning curve" to dramatically increase your output and your productivity. Bunch your tasks and do several of the same type of tasks all at the same time. The more of a similar task you do, the less time it takes you to do each subsequent task.

For example, if you write all of your reports or proposals one after another, you will become faster and more efficient as you work. It will take you less time to do each one. If you make all your phone calls at once, each call will take less time and be more efficient.

Utilize the "experience curve" as well to rise to the top of your field. The better you get at a job, the more of that job you can do at a higher level of quality and in a shorter period of time.

The combination of the learning curve and the experience curve will make you one of the most productive and valuable people in your organization.

How you can apply this law immediately:

1. Be absolutely clear about the most important tasks that you do in terms of reward and recognition in your work. Organize your time so that you are doing more of these tasks, doing them together, and getting more of them done sooner.

2. Get better at the key skills or core competencies that enable you to do your job in an excellent fashion. How can you get better and better at performing the most important tasks required by your work?

98. The Law of Time Pressure

—∞—

There is never enough time to do everything,
but there is always enough time to do the
most important things.

When you find yourself under pressure to get a job done by a particular deadline, you are forced to be vastly more efficient than you would ever be if you felt that you had ample time. This explains why so many people get the job done only when they are faced with stringent deadlines.

Parkinson's Law says, "Work expands to fill the time allotted for it." If you have two hours of work to do and an entire day in which to do it, the work will tend to expand gradually, and will take you all day long to complete the two hours of work.

However, the reverse is also true. It is "Work contracts to fill the time allotted for it." Use this law by setting deadlines for yourself that force you to complete the task far sooner. Continually analyze your work and focus your attention on completing your most important task, the task that represents the most valuable contribution you can make, on schedule, if not before.

Here are four questions you can ask yourself every day to keep yourself focused on your most important tasks:

1. What are my *highest value activities?* What are the things I do that contribute the greatest amount of value to my work?

2. What are my *key result areas?* What are the specific results that I have been hired to accomplish?

3. Why am I *on the payroll?* Why do they pay me money at my job? What specifically have I been tasked to do?

4. What can I and only I do that, if done well, will make a *real difference?* If I don't do it, it won't get done. But if I do it, and I do it well, it will make a significant contribution to my work and my life. What is it?

At any given time, there is usually only one activity that represents the highest and best use of your time. Your job is to identify it and then to throw your whole heart into getting it done quickly and well.

How you can apply this law immediately:

1. Identify your most important tasks, the tasks that represent the most significant contribution you make to your company. Resolve to work exclusively on those tasks before you start on anything else.

2. Create your own "forcing system." Set specific deadlines for yourself and then resolve to get the job done well ahead of schedule.

99. The Law of Single Handling

—‌ɯ—

The ability to start and complete your most important task determines your productivity more than any other skill.

Maximum performance is possible only when you concentrate single-mindedly on one task, the most important task, and you stay at it until it is 100 percent complete.

You cannot do everything, but you can do *one* thing, the most important thing, and you can do it now. By setting goals and priorities, and then by selecting your most important task, you can dramatically increase your level of productivity and output.

Single handling is perhaps the most powerful of all time management techniques. It can increase your output by as much as 500 percent. It can reduce the amount of time you spend on a task by fully 80 percent—by the very act of launching into the task and disciplining yourself to stay with it until it is complete.

Picking up a task, putting it down, and coming back to it several times dramatically increases the amount of time necessary to complete the task. On the other hand, picking up the task and refusing to put it down until it is done enables you to accomplish vastly more in a shorter period of time than you thought possible. By disciplining yourself to concentrate single-mindedly on the most important thing you could possibly be doing, and then by completing that task, you increase the quantity, quality, and value of your output substantially.

You can have all the talent and skill in the world. But if you cannot discipline yourself single-mindedly to complete your most important task, you will always have to work for someone else. You will always have to be supervised by someone who can make sure that you do what you should do, when you should do it.

The good news is that every time you complete a major task, you experience a surge of energy, enthusiasm, and self-esteem. You feel terrific about yourself. You feel happy and elated. You feel like a winner.

The more important the task and the more disciplined you are in completing the task, the better you feel about yourself when you have finished.

By assigning yourself a large task and then by disciplining yourself to concentrate single-mindedly until the task is complete, you eventually develop the all-important habit of *task completion*. You program your subconscious mind in such a way that you look forward to major tasks because you know how good you are going to feel when you have completed them.

How you can apply this law immediately:

1. Resolve today to develop the lifelong habit of task completion. You do this by selecting your most important task, getting yourself organized, and then working on it wholeheartedly until it is complete. Do this over and over until this habit of single handling is firmly entrenched.

2. Identify the biggest and most important single task or project that you have facing you right now. Whatever it is, clear aside everything else and throw your whole heart into completing it, no matter how long it takes.

   When you are working on your most important task, anything else you could do is a relative waste of time. No matter what else comes up, you will have the satisfaction of knowing that there is nothing more important than what you are doing at this moment. This is the key to high productivity and great success.

100. The Law of Competence

—∞—

You can increase your efficiency and your effectiveness by becoming better and better at your key tasks.

One of the most powerful of all time management techniques is for you to get *better* at the most important things you do. Your core competencies, your key skill areas, the places where you are absolutely excellent at what you do, are the key determinants of your productivity, your standard of living, and the level of achievement you reach in your field.

The market pays excellent rewards only for excellent work. You are therefore successful to the degree to which you do more things better than the average person. Your great responsibility in life is to determine what things you can and should do very well and then to develop a plan to become very, very good in those vital areas.

Here is the key question again: What one skill, if you developed and did it in an excellent fashion, would have the greatest positive impact on your career?

Your weakest important skill sets the height at which you can use all your other skills. Be honest with yourself. What is your limiting skill? What is the one skill that determines the speed at which you complete your major tasks and achieve your goals? What is the one skill, the lack of which may be holding you back?

The Pareto Principle, the 80/20 Rule, applies to those skills that are limiting your success. Eighty percent of the reasons you are not moving ahead as fast as you want is explained by the 20 percent of skills and abilities that you lack.

This rule also says that 80 percent of your limits in life are contained within yourself. Eighty percent of the reasons you are not achieving your goals as quickly as you want is because of the lack of a particular skill, ability, or quality within yourself.

The underachiever always looks for the reasons for his or her problems in the outer world. The high achiever looks within. The high-achieving person always asks, What is it in me that is holding me back?

Successful people look into themselves for the answers to their questions and for the solutions to their problems. Unsuccessful people always look outside. Who do you think finds the solutions first?

How you can apply this law immediately:

1. Identify your key result areas and your core competencies. What are the most important things you do in your work and how well do you do them? Give yourself a score of one to ten on each one, with one being the lowest and ten being the highest in terms of how good you are in that area.

2. Ask people around you to evaluate you in your critical skill areas on a scale of one to ten. The more accurate you can be about this exercise, the easier it will be for you to focus on the one or two skill areas that can help you the most.

3. Identify the one skill, the most important skill, the one that, if you developed and did it in an excellent fashion, would have the greatest positive impact on your career. Whatever it is, set a goal, make a plan, and go to work to become excellent in that area. You will be absolutely amazed at the difference it will make in your career.

Summary

The principles of time management have been known and practiced by highly productive people throughout history, in every organization and in every field of endeavor. They are the basic laws of life management. They are immutable and unchanging. And they work to enable you to be vastly more successful than you could ever imagine being without them.

The best news of all is that the rules for business success are not complicated or difficult to understand. They are really quite simple and easy to apply. They simply require the four *D*s to make them your own for the rest of your career.

The first *D* is *Desire*. This is the starting point of all great personal or professional achievement. You must really, really want your goals. You must be willing to make the necessary efforts to develop these time management habits until they become a part of your personality and your character.

The second *D* stands for *Decision*. You must get off the fence. You must make a clear, unequivocal decision that you are going to practice these behaviors and develop these habits no matter how long it takes.

The third *D* is *Discipline*. This is the most important single quality you can develop for lifelong success and great personal achievement. With a highly developed sense of personal discipline, you can conquer the world. Without it, very little is possible.

The fourth *D* stands for *Determination*. This is the one great quality that enables you to overcome all setbacks, disappointments, temporary failures, and every obstacle that life throws in your path. Your determination, your persistence, is your measure of your belief in yourself.

There are really no limits on what you can accomplish with your life except for the limits you place on yourself by your own thinking.

Start Now!

—◇◇◇—

Where do you begin? You have learned 100 laws and more than 200 corollaries of these laws. You have read hundreds of action steps you can take to implement and apply these laws to your life. What do you do now?

Theodore Roosevelt once said, "Do what you can, with what you have, right where you are."

What matters, more than anything, is that you take action on at least one idea that can help you immediately. Don't delay or procrastinate. If you think that you can improve your life, work, or personal effectiveness with a particular action step, just do it.

Fully 95 percent of everything you do is determined by your habits, good or bad. A habit is an automatic, conditioned response or ritual of personal or business life. Your great goal is to form good habits that then function on their own, enhancing the quality of your life and increasing the scope of your rewards.

Begin by deciding today exactly what you really want in life. Write out a list of your goals for the years ahead. And don't be cautious or careful.

Set big goals—goals that excite and inspire you—and make definite, written plans for their accomplishment. Create schedules and set deadlines. Make your activities and accomplishments measurable, and then take action!

Action orientation is the most outwardly identifiable quality of a winning human being. The world is full of people who are mentally vacationing on "Someday I'll." They are always planning, preparing, and thinking about what they're going to do "someday." Don't you be one of them.

Perhaps the greatest quality you can develop in business is a "sense of urgency," what Tom Peters calls "a bias for action." Only about 2 percent of people have developed the habit of moving quickly when opportunity or danger presents itself. And these people tend to move to the front of every line, of every organization or area of endeavor.

Thomas Edison wrote, "Good things come to those who wait, but only what's left over from those who hustle."

When you think, decide, and take action on one single idea, you are a much better person than someone who learns hundreds of ideas but who does nothing.

The good news is that the faster you move, the more experiences you have and the more lessons you learn.

The faster you move, the smarter and more capable you become. The faster you move, the more ground you cover, the more people you meet, the more opportunities you discover, and the more doors open for you.

The faster you move, the more energy you have and the more enthusiastic and confident you become.

The faster you move, the more creative and competent you become in any area. The faster you move, the more you get done and the more capable you become of doing even more.

Nothing succeeds like success. When you learn and apply these ideas every day, you develop the deep-down habit of action orientation. And the more you "try," the more you will "tri-umph."

You move from "positive thinking" to "positive knowing." You move from wishing and hoping to an absolute conviction that you can do anything you put your mind to.

You are an extraordinary person. You have talents and abilities far beyond anything you have ever accomplished. You are living in the Golden Age of humankind, where more achievements are possible for more people than have ever been imagined before.

There are no limits on what you can do, be, or have except for the limits you place on your own mind. Go for it!

Learning Resources of
Brian Tracy International

—ᲛᲛ—

Brian Tracy
Speaker, Trainer, Seminar Leader

Brian Tracy is one of the top professional speakers in the world, addressing more than 300,000 people each year throughout the United States, Europe, Asia, and Australia.

Brian's keynote speeches, talks, and seminars are described as "inspiring, entertaining, informative, and motivational." His audiences include Fortune 500 companies and every size of business and association.

Call today for full information on booking Brian to speak at your next meeting or conference.

21st Century Thinking—How to outthink, outplan, and outstrategize your competition and get superior results in a turbulent, fast-changing business environment.

Advanced Selling Strategies—How to outthink, outperform, and outsell your competition using the most advanced strategies and tactics known to modern selling.

The Psychology of Success—How the top people think and act in every area of personal and business life. Countless practical, proven methods and strategies for peak performance.

Leadership in the New Millennium—How to apply the most powerful leadership principles ever discovered to manage, motivate, and get better results, faster, than ever before.

Brian will carefully customize his talk for you and for your needs. Please call 858/481-2977 today for a free promotional package.

Personal Coaching from Brian Tracy

Brian Tracy's Focal Point Advanced Coaching and Mentoring System

- **Personal Strategic Planning • Improved Performance**
- **Greater Focus and Clarity • Balance in Life**
- **Greater Earnings • Less Work**
- **How to Concentrate on Highest Value Activities**
- **Mastermind Network • Ongoing Evaluation and Review**
- **Achieving Goals Faster**

The Focal Point System is designed for successful entrepreneurs, executives, and sales professionals who want to move to the next level in their careers and personal lives.

This group coaching program takes place four times each year in San Diego, California. Participants complete preliminary work before each session. You learn how to design your own personal strategic plan; how to implement your plan with daily, weekly, and monthly blueprints; and how to upgrade your plan as you move forward.

Coaching sessions are small and personal with ample opportunity for interaction and brainstorming with other successful people and for personal planning.

Result: you will double your income (or more) and simplify your life, increasing your time off, over the two- to three-year program.

To register, or for complete details, visit our Web site at **www.briantracy.com** or phone Brian Tracy International at **858/481-2977**. Write to Brian Tracy International, 462 Stevens Avenue, Suite 202, Solana Beach, California 92075 or fax to 858/481-2445.

Brian Tracy Audio Learning Programs

	Audio	CD
Psychology of Achievement (7 hours) The most popular program on success and achievement in the world.	$65.00	$70.00
Psychology of Success (7 hours) The 10 principles of peak performance practiced by all high achievers.	$65.00	$70.00
Psychology of Selling (7 hours) The most powerful, practical, professional selling program in the world today.	$75.00	$80.00
How to Master Your Time (7 hours) More than 500 key ideas for time management in a proven system that brings about immediate results. Save 2 hours every day.	$65.00	$70.00
Million-Dollar Habits (7 hours) The specific habits and behaviors practiced by high earners and self-made millionaires. Double and triple your income.	$65.00	$70.00
How Leaders Lead (7 hours) With Ken Blanchard. How to manage, motivate, inspire, and lead a winning team.	$65.00	$70.00
Advanced Selling Techniques (7 hours) The most complete advanced selling program for top professionals in the world.	$75.00	$80.00
Master Strategies for High Achievement (7 hours) More than 150 of the key strategies practiced by the most successful people—in every area of life.	$65.00	$70.00

Accelerated Learning Techniques (7 hours) How to learn faster, remember more, unlock the power of your mind for maximum performance.	**$65.00**	**$70.00**
Thinking Big (7 hours) How to dream big dreams, build self-confidence, set goals, develop the mind-set of successful people.	**$65.00**	**$70.00**
The Luck Factor (7 hours) More than 60 proven strategies to increase the likelihood that you will be the right person at the right place at the right time to succeed greatly.	**$65.00**	**$70.00**
Breaking the Success Barrier (7 hours) The 12 most powerful thinking tools ever discovered enable you to overcome any obstacle, achieve any goal.	**$65.00**	**$70.00**

Special offer:
Any 1 program = $65;
2–3 programs = $60 each;
4–5 programs = $55 each;
any 6 programs = $295;
any 10 programs = $475.

To order one or more of these programs, phone 800/542-4252 or visit our Web site at www.briantracy.com. You may write to Brian Tracy International, 462 Stevens Avenue, Suite 202, Solana Beach, CA 92075. Our fax number is 858-481-2445.

Unconditionally Guaranteed for ONE FULL YEAR!

If you are not delighted with these learning programs, you can return the materials for a complete refund anytime in the year following the date of purchase.

High Performance Leadership

The most advanced and complete multimedia Executive Development Program for managers in the world today.

Learn how to build, manage, or turn around any business. You learn how to set strategies, plan, organize, and get superior results. You learn how to interview, recruit, delegate, supervise, manage, motivate, and build a top team of dedicated employees.

The program consists of twenty-four video-based sessions plus detailed workbooks for participant follow-up and reinforcement.

Seminar sessions include
• Becoming a Leader • Strategies for Effective Leadership • Entrepreneurial Thinking • How Excellent Leaders Lead • The Key Functions of Managers • The Pursuit of Personal Excellence • Seven Secrets of Managerial Success • Superior Selection Skills • Delegation 6 the Key to Leverage • The Customer is Always Right • Becoming a Master of Change • How to Solve Every Problem • Setting Your Priorities • Building Peak Performance Teams • Communicate With Power • A Great Place to Work • Motivating People for Maximum Results • Getting the Best Out of Others • Fielding a Winning Team • Coping With Difficult People • Inspecting What You Expect • Boosting Employee Performance • Negotiating Strategies and Tactics • Making the Best Decisions

This program is offered to individuals and organizations through our national network of trained consultants and facilitators.

For complete details, call **800/542-4252** or visit our Web site at **www.briantracy.com**. Write to Brian Tracy International, 462 Stevens Avenue, Suite 202, Solana Beach, California 92075.

Successful Selling

The most complete multimedia training program on advanced selling in the world today. Thirty video-based sessions with a workbook and application exercises.

You can double and triple your sales with the powerful, practical, proven principles and techniques you learn in this program.

Seminar sessions include

The Winning Edge • Qualities of Top Salespeople • The New Model of Selling • Mega-Credibility in Selling • Asking Your Way to Success • Secrets of Success in Selling • Overcoming Price Resistance • Closing the Sale • Psychology of Selling • Time Management for Salespeople • Influencing Customer Behavior • How Buyers Buy • Selling Made Simple • Selling Different People Differently • Power, Politics, and Influence • Value-Added Selling • Selling Consultatively • Prospecting Power • Complex Selling • Personal Sales Planning • Relationship Selling • Selling on Nonprice Issues • Negotiating the Sale • Identifying Needs and Presenting Solutions • Qualities of Top Negotiators • Building Customer Relationships • Overcoming Objections • Customers for Life • Telephone Sales • Service Excellence

This entire training program is only $1,995 and is designed for ease of use and self-administration. Each graduate receives a diploma upon completion.

To purchase this program, call **800/542-4252** or visit our Web site at **www.briantracy.com**. Write to Brian Tracy International, 462 Stevens Avenue, Suite 202, Solana Beach, California 92075.

Unconditionally Guaranteed for ONE FULL YEAR!

If you are not delighted with this learning program, you can return the materials for a complete refund any time in the year following the date of purchase.

Maximum Performance

This is the most complete program for increasing individual productivity, performance, and output in the world.

In thirty fast-moving, impactful sessions, participants learn how to plan their work better, set goals, manage their time, solve problems, think creatively, work as teams, communicate clearly, and get more done than ever before.

This multimedia corporate learning program includes thirty videos and a workbook for follow-up and reinforcement plus complete step-by-step instructions for use in any organization.

Seminar sessions include

Seven Secrets of Success • Your 1000 Percent Formula • The Race Is On • Five Steps to Goal Setting • Setting Your Priorities • Fast-Tracking Your Career • Seven Steps to Mental Fitness • Five Keys to Personal Power • Developing Personal Power • Programming Yourself for Success • Leveraging Your Potential • Reengineering Your Life • Being a Better Communicator • Negotiation Skills • The Three Cs of Success • Choices and Consequences • Effective Decision-Making • Balancing Your Life • Making It a GREAT Life • Getting Mentors for Success • The Business of Life • Dream Big Dreams • Critical Factors of Success • Becoming an Unshakable Optimist • Stop Worrying, Start Living • The High Road to Achievement • The Luck Factor • Designing Your Future • Thinking Big • Character Counts

The cost of this complete program is $1,995 plus $97 per additional student workbook.

To purchase this program, call direct at **800/542-4252** or visit our Web site at **www.briantracy.com**. Write to Brian Tracy International, 462 Stevens Avenue, Suite 202, Solana Beach, California 92075.

Unconditionally Guaranteed for ONE FULL YEAR!

If you are not delighted with this learning program, you can return the materials for a complete refund any time in the year following the date of purchase.

Recommended Reading

—m—

The Achievement Factors. B. Eugene Griessman.

The Achiever's Profile. Allan Cox.

Achieving Peak Performance. Nido Qubein.

The Acorn Principle. Jim Cathcart.

Advanced Selling Strategies. Brian Tracy.

Adversity Quotient. Paul G. Stolz.

The Art of Negotiating. Gerald Nierenberg.

Breakpoint and Beyond. George Land and Beth Jarman.

Breathing Space. Jeff Davidson.

Built to Last. James C. Collins and Jerry I. Porras.

The Business of Selling. Tony Alessandra and Jim Cathcart.

Competing in the Third Wave. Jeremy Hope and Tony Hope.

Consultative Selling. Mack Hanan.

Creating Wealth. Robert G. Allen.

Creating Your Future. George Morrisey.

Customer Intimacy. Fred Wiersema.

Customers for Life. Carl Sewell.

Do What You Love, the Money Will Follow. Marsha Sinetar.

Economics in One Lesson. Henry Hazlitt.

The Effective Executive. Peter F. Drucker.

Essays. Ralph Waldo Emerson.

The Experience Economy. B. Joseph Tine II and James H. Gilmore.

Fast-Growth Management. Mack Hanan.

Faust. Johann Wolfgang von Goethe.

The Feldman Method. Ben Feldman.

The Fifth Discipline. Peter Senge.

Flow: The Psychology of Optimal Experience. Mihalay Csiksczentmihalyi.

Getting Everything You Can out of All You've Got. Jay Abraham.

The Great American Success Story. George Gallup Jr. and Alec N. Gallup.

Henderson on Corporate Strategy. Bruce Henderson.

How to Win Customers. Heinz Goldman.

Hyper Growth. H. Skip Weitzen.

Innovation and Entrepreneurship. Peter F. Drucker.

Job Shift. William Bridges.

Key Management Ideas. Stuart Crainer.

The Law of Success. Napoleon Hill.

Leadership. James J. Cribbin.

The Leadership Challenge. James M. Kouzes and Barry C. Posner.

Leadership When the Heat's On. Danny Cox.

Leading People. Robert H. Rosen.

Life beyond Time Management. Kim Norup and Willy Norup.

Lifetime Guide to Money. Wall Street Journal.

Locus of Control. Herbert M. Lefcourt.

The Management of Time. James T. McKay.

Managing for Results. Peter F. Drucker.

Managing the Future. Robert B. Tucker.

Man's Search for Meaning. Victor Frankl.

The Marketing Imagination. Theodore Leavitt.

Maximum Achievement. Brian Tracy.

Megatrends 2000. John Naisbitt and Patricia Aburdene.

Million Dollar Habits. Robert Ringer.

The Negotiators' Handbook. George Fuller.

Nicomachian Ethics. Aristotle.

Nobody Gets Rich Working for Somebody Else. Roger Fritz.

Og Mandino's University of Success. Og Mandino.

On Becoming a Leader. Warren Bennis.

Only the Paranoid Survive. Andrew S. Grove.

The Organized Executive. Stephanie Winston.

Organized to Be the Best. Susan Silver.

Outperformers. Mack Hanan.

Passion for Excellence. Tom Peters and Nancy Austin.

The Path of Least Resistance. Robert Fritz.

Pathfinders. Gayle Sheehy.

Peak Performers. Charles Garfield.

Permission Marketing. Seth Godin.

Play to Win. Larry Wilson.

Positioning. Al Reis and Jack Trout.

Power in Management. John P. Cotter.

The Power of Purpose. Richard J. Leider.

The Power of Simplicity. Jack Trout.

The Practice of Management. Peter F. Drucker.

Price Wars. Thomas J. Winninger.

Profit Patterns. Adrian J. Slywotzky and David J. Morrison.

Pushing the Envelope. Harvey Mackay.

Pygmalion in the Classroom. Dr. Robert Rosenthal.

Quality Is Free. Phillip Crosby.

Quality without Tears. Phillip Crosby.

Real Time. Regis McKenna.

Relationship Selling. Jim Cathcart.

The Richest Man in Babylon. George Classon.

The Sale. Don Hutson.

Secrets of Effective Leadership. F. A. Manske Jr.

Sell Easy. Thomas J. Winninger.

Selling the Invisible. Harry Beckwith.

Servant Leadership. Robert K. Greenleaf.

The Seven Habits of Highly Effective People. Stephen Covey.

The Situational Leader. Dr. Paul Hersey.

The Soul of a Business. Tom Chappell.

Stress without Distress. Hans Selye.

Success Is a Journey. Brian Tracy.

The Success Principle. Ronald N. Yeaple.

TechnoTrends. Daniel Burrus.

The Unheavenly City. Dr. Edward Banfield.

Think and Grow Rich. Napoleon Hill.

The Time Trap. Alex McKenzie.

Top Management Strategy. Benjamin B. Tregoe and John W. Zimmerman.

The 22 Immutable Laws of Branding. Al Reis and Laura Reis.

The 22 Immutable Laws of Marketing. Al Reis and Jack Trout.

Visionary Leadership. Bert Mannus.

Visions. Ty Boyd.

Wealth without Risk. Charles J. Givens.

Working Smart. Michael LeBoeuf.

You Can Negotiate Anything. Herb Cohen.

The Zurich Axioms. Max Gunther.

Index

—m—

Value, 18, 273, 287. *See also* Most
    Valuable Asset, Law of
  money as measure of, 158
  subjective, 230
Values, 141, 142. *See also* Integrity,
    Law of
Victim, feeling like, 224
Vision, 133–135
Visualization, 134
  of perfect life, 25
Volunteering, 40

Wake Up and Live (Brande), 62
Walk Away Law, 262–263
Walt Disney Corporation, 82–83
Walton, Sam, 86
Watson, Thomas J., Sr., 124
Weaknesses
  assessing, 127, 128
  personal, 100
Wealth. *See also* Financial indepen-
    dence; Money; Prosperity;
    Rich people
  decision to achieve, 156
  deserving, 154
Welch, Jack, 107, 126
Weldon, Joel, 57
What They Still Don't Teach You at the
    Harvard Business School
    (McCormick), 30

Win-WIn or No Deal, Law of,
  235–237
Winning, thinking about, 145
"Winning Edge," 2
Winning through Intimidation
    (Ringer), 255
Wording and word choice, 218, 222
Work. *See also specific topics*
  achievements amenable to hard,
    52–54
  adding greater value to one's, 55,
    56, 159
Work hours/work week, 52–54
Work schedule, organizing one's, 54
Work tasks and accomplishments,
    162–163. *See also* Task com-
    pletion

Xerox, 217

Yahoo, 107
Yearning years, 174

Zero-based thinking, 264–265
Ziglar, Zig, 198